天津历史风貌建筑

HISTORIC ARCHITECTURE IN TIANJIN

天津市历史风貌建筑保护专家咨询委员会
天 津 市 保 护 风 貌 建 筑 办 公 室 主编

TIANJIN PROFESSIONAL CONSULTING COMMITTEE FOR THE PROTECTION OF HISTORIC ARCHITECTURE
TIANJIN PROTECTION OFFICE OF HISTORIC AND STYLISTIC BUILDING

天津大学出版社
TIANJIN UNIVERSITY PRESS

《天津历史风貌建筑》编写组
WRITING GROUP

主　　编：路　红
副 主 编：徐连和　孙　超　舒德庆　傅建华　张俊东
顾　　问：邹德侬　罗澍伟　夏　青
编　　辑：李琦琳　孔　晖　陈广发　谈卫卫　袁　勇　肖　楠　李　莉
　　　　　姚　鑫　何效星　唐　晓　曹　宇
摄　　影：何　方　何　易　金　研　刘锦标

Editor-in-chief: Lu Hong
Associate Editors: Xu Lianhe, Sun Chao, Shu Deqing, Fu Jianhua, Zhang Jundong
Consultants: Zou Denong, Luo Shuwei, Xia Qing
Editors: Li Qilin, Kong Hui, Chen Guangfa, Tan Weiwei, Yuan Yong,
Xiao Nan, Li Li, Yao Xin, He Xiaoxing, Tang Xiao, Cao Yu
Photographers: He Fang, He Yi, Jin Yan, Liu Jinbiao

主编单位：天津市历史风貌建筑保护专家咨询委员会　天津市保护风貌建筑办公室
承编单位：《中国建筑文化遗产》编辑部

Organizer: Tianjin Professional Consulting Committee for the Protection of Historic Architecture, Tianjin Protection Office of Historic and Stylistic Building
Operator: *China Architectural Heritage* Editorial Office

目 录

CONTENTS

天津历史风貌建筑保护概况

天津市历史风貌建筑保护专家咨询委员会
路红[1]

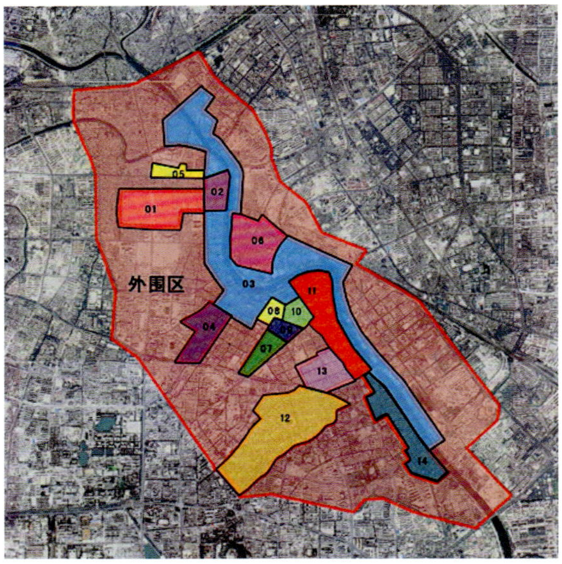

14片历史文化图
14 protective areas of historical and cultural heritages

01. 老城厢历史文化街区	Seat of the Old City Area
02. 古文化街历史文化街区	Ancient Cultural Street Area
03. 海河历史文化街区	Haihe River Area
04. 鞍山道历史文化街区	Anshan Avenue Area
05. 估衣街历史文化街区	Gu Yi Street Area
06. 一宫花园历史文化街区	Yigong Garden Area
07. 赤峰道历史文化街区	Chifeng Avenue Area
08. 劝业场历史文化街区	Quan ye cheng Mall Area
09. 中心花园历史文化街区	Central Garden Area
10. 承德道历史文化街区	Chengde Avenue Area
11. 解放北路历史文化街区	North Jiefang Road Area
12. 五大道历史文化街区	The Five Avenues Area
13. 泰安道历史文化街区	Taian Avenue Area
14. 解放南路历史文化街区	South Jiefang Road Area

一、基本情况

历史风貌建筑是天津保护特定建筑遗产的法定名词，按照《天津市历史风貌建筑保护条例》的定位，历史风貌建筑是："建成50年以上，在建筑样式、结构、施工工艺和工程技术等方面具有建筑艺术特色和科学价值；反映本市历史文化和民俗传统特点，具有时代特色和地域特色；具有异国建筑风格特点；著名建筑师的代表作品；在革命发展史上具有特殊纪念意义；在产业发展史上具有代表性的作坊、商铺、厂房和仓库；名人故居及其他具有特殊历史意义的建筑"。

2005年9月1日，《天津市历史风貌建筑保护条例》（以下简称《条例》）实施，按照《条例》的规定，经天津市历史风貌建筑保护专家咨询委员会审查、社会公示，天津市政府于2005-2013年分6批确认了历史风貌建筑877幢、126万平方米。其中，特殊保护级别69幢，重点保护级别205幢，一般保护级别603幢，分布在全市15个区县。在877幢历史风貌建筑中，有部分各级文物保护单位。

1986年天津市被确定为国家级历史文化名城，2006年3月国务院批准的天津市城市总体规划的历史文化名城规划中，确定了14片历史文化街区，大部分历史风貌建筑就坐落在这些历史文化街区内。

天津现存的历史风貌建筑既有中国传统风格的四合院、殿堂、寺院，又有西洋古典、现代建筑，它们和历史文化风貌保护区一起，形成了独特的建筑文化和城市景观，也是天津作为国家级历史文化名城的重要载体。

1 路红，天津市规划和自然资源局原一级巡视员，天津市历史风貌建筑保护专家咨询委员会第一、第二、第三届主任。

二、历史背景

天津的历史风貌建筑和历史风貌保护区是天津社会和城市发展的见证。天津地区发现最早的人类活动遗存，属距今一万年前的旧石器时代；隋唐、宋辽时期，天津地区出现了规模较大的人类聚居地和建筑群。目前人类建筑活动的最早实物为重建于辽代统和二年（984年）的独乐寺。明永乐二年（1404年）天津设卫，明成祖朱棣为纪念自己南下夺取政权之事，赐名“天津”，即天子的渡口，由此开始了天津的城市历史。

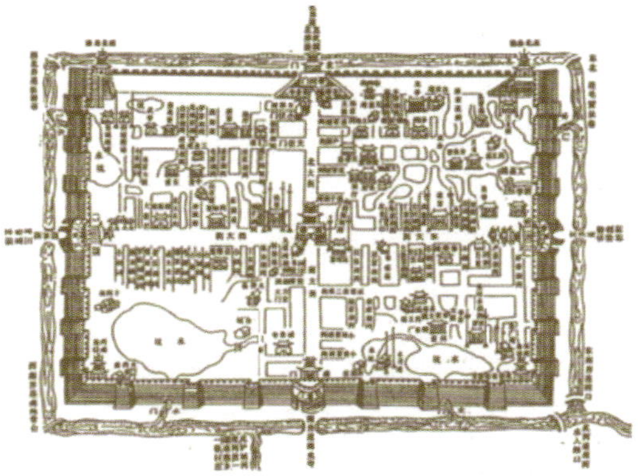

天津老城厢图
The map of the old town of Tianjin

历经明清两朝，天津以老城厢为建筑的大本营，以漕运文化为基础，经历了由卫城到州城、府城的升级，也逐渐地由单纯的军事基地演变成为商贾云集的中国北方经济文化重镇。天津老城城池为长方形，占地约1.76平方千米，与中国传统古城基本类似，平面是以鼓楼为中心的十字街布局，四条大道两侧配以小街、小巷，形成若干胡同街坊，老城建筑除少数公署衙门、文庙等为传统大式建筑外，民居以小式建筑为主，杂以部分南方民居形式，呈现了南北交融的中国传统建筑风格。

明代鼓楼
The Drum Tower of Ming Dynasty

1860年第二次鸦片战争后，天津被迫开埠；1900年八国联军入侵，天津老城于1900年11月26日被八国联军拆毁，四段城墙改成了四条马路。从1860年开始，英、法、美、德、日、俄、意大利、比利时、奥匈帝国等9个帝国主义国家先后在天津设立了租界，天津九国租界的形成大致分为三个阶段。

第一阶段：英、法、美租界的开辟。1860年，英法联军发动的第二次鸦片战争迫使清政府签订了中英、中法《北京条约》，天津开埠成为通商口岸。同年12月7日，划海河西岸紫竹林、下园一带为英租界；次年6月，法、美两国亦在英租界南北分别设立租界。

第二阶段：德、日租界的开辟与英租界的扩张。首先，德国于1895年在海河西岸开辟租界。1896年日本在法租界以西开辟租界。1897年，英国强行将其原租界扩张到南京路北侧。

第三阶段：九国租界的形成。1900年八国联军入侵，俄国于1900年在海河东岸划定租界，比利时于1902年在俄租界之南划租界地，意大利也于同年在俄租界之北开辟租界，最后奥匈帝国在意租界以北占地为租界。与此同时，英、法、日、德四国又趁机扩充其租界地，最后形成了九国

广东会馆
The Guangdong provincial guildhall

租界聚集海河两岸，总计占地23 350.5亩（约1 556.7公顷）的格局。而当时的天津老城厢占地2 940亩（约196公顷），仅为租界地的1/8。

九国租界在天津存续时间最长的为英租界——85年，最短的为奥匈租界——17年。九国租界并存同一城市，在世界城市的发展史上是空前的。由此可见天津在中国近代史上负载了最沉重的耻辱，同时九国租界遗存的历史风貌建筑及其建设过程中派生的多元文化，也成为今天城市建设中不可忽视的历史文脉和宝贵的文化资源。大规模的租界建设，使得西洋建筑文化和技术涌入天津，天津的建筑从中国传统形式走向了中西荟萃、百花齐放的形式。

在中国城市发展史上，600多年的城市仍是年轻的城市。天津作为国家级历史文化名城，没有北京、西安、南京等古都的显赫地位，也没有扬州、苏州、开封等古城的辉煌文化，天津城市文化的突出价值在于明清两朝依托大运河发展的河海文化、近代百年城市与西方文明的对接，鸦片战争后中国发生的重大历史事件大部分能在天津找到痕迹，因此在中国史学界，素有“五千年看西安，一千年看北京，近代中国看天津”的说法。

三、基本类型

天津的历史风貌建筑林林总总，跨越了1 000多年，涵盖了居住、公共建筑等多个领域。为便于管理和研究，我们从三个方面进行分类。

（一）按建筑年代分类

1860年第二次鸦片战争后，天津被迫开埠，逐渐成为9个帝国主义国家的租界，天津的建筑从中国式传统建筑走向了中西荟萃，突出地表现了时代的变迁和观念的转换，有很强的时代标记。因此我们以1860年为分水岭，将天津的历史风貌建筑主要分为古代历史风貌建筑（1860年以前）和近代历史风貌建筑（1860年以后）。

古代历史风貌建筑主要为中国传统式建筑，现存50余幢，主要分布在蓟州、老城厢。如建于辽代统和二年（984年）的独乐寺、元朝泰定三年（1326年）的天后宫、明朝初年（1427年）的玉皇阁。

近代历史风貌建筑是天津历史风貌建筑中数量最多、

最具特色的瑰宝，主要分布在天津市中心城区海河两岸。

（二）按使用功能分为十类

居住建筑是目前保存量最大也最具特色的一类，其中又可细分为独立式住宅、单元公寓式住宅、独门联排式住宅等。其他类型为教育建筑、金融建筑、商贸建筑、办公建筑、厂房仓库、宗教建筑、娱乐体育建筑、医院建筑、交通建筑等。

（三）按建筑的外部特征分为五类

中国传统官式建筑：指严格按照中国传统建筑的形制建造的建筑，主要为寺庙、官衙等，如天后宫、玉皇阁、大悲院等。

欧洲古典复兴主义特征：建筑多以古希腊、古罗马及文艺复兴时期的建筑范式为摹本，如原开滦矿务局办公楼、原汇丰银行等。

折中主义特征：既有欧洲典型的集仿主义建筑，又有中西合璧的折中主义建筑，天津大多数历史风貌建筑属于此类，如鲍贵卿旧宅等。

各国民居特征：由中国传统民居和天津地方文化结合产生的天津合院民居形式，如石家大院、徐家大院等；更多的是采用欧洲各国的典型民居形式，如西班牙、英国、德国、意大利等国的民居。

现代主义特征：引进新结构、新材料的建筑，如利华大楼、渤海大楼等。

四、基本特点

（一）建筑年代相对集中

天津60%的历史风貌建筑是在1900–1937 年不到40年的时间里建成的。

（二）各类建筑相对集中，呈现群区性

中国传统建筑集中在老城厢和古文化街一带；建筑规模宏大的金融建筑主要集中在解放北路一带，被称为“金融一条街”；商贸性建筑主要集中在和平路及估衣街、古文化街一带；居住建筑主要集中在老城厢、河北区一宫、河西区大营门、和平区五大道地区及中心花园附近；仓库建筑则集中在海河沿岸。

独门独院住宅——张园
A separated mansion — Zhangyuan Garden

单元公寓式住宅——民园大楼
An apartment building — the Minyuan Building

独门联排式住宅——安乐邨
A suite of flats with separated entrances in a block — Anle Village

鲍贵卿旧宅
The former residence of Bao Guiqing

达文士小楼（西班牙风格）
The Davinci villa (Spanish style)

许氏住宅（英国风格）
The Xu's Family residence (British style)

利华大楼
Leopold Building

（三）近代历史风貌建筑的设计理念、应用技术与西方社会同步

一是先进的设计理念：20世纪20年代，正值英国“花园城市”规划理论盛行之时，英租界新区（即现在的五大道地区）基本按照该理论进行规划与建设，居住区规模适中，配备了学校、教堂、花园、体育场等完整的公共配套设施，形成了宜人的空间尺度和舒适的居住环境。新型公寓建筑、联排住宅等也直接从其诞生地移植到了天津。

二是完善的公共配套和室内设施：各租界的建设注重整地筑路，建设完善的市政设施，如路灯、绿化、排水等设施的建设，在住宅中引进推广了水冲式厕所，改善了居住环境，提高了卫生水平。

三是先进的房地产开发模式：各租界的建设引进了西方的房地产开发理念和模式。如英法租界将地块按照四方块划分，周围用道路围合，利于分期出让土地。

四是现代生活方式和城市空间：各租界的建设引进了西方的现代生活方式，如以起居、餐厅、舞厅为中心的家庭生活方式，以公园、教堂、市政厅为中心的社会生活方式，以电车、汽车代步的现代交通方式。这些开放的生活方式与封闭的中国传统方式迥然不同，同时也带来了截然不同的城市空间。

（四）建筑风格纷呈，建筑艺术多样

由于受中国传统建筑和西方建筑思潮的双重影响，形成了中国传统建筑、古典复兴建筑、折中主义建筑、现代建筑等不同风格建筑共存的局面。它们相互辉映，共同形成了天津独特而又丰富的城市空间和景观。

（五）建筑材料及建造技术特色突出

天津独特的地理环境和水土，形成了独特的建筑材料和建造技术，这些材料和技术在历史风貌建筑上得到了充分体现。如黏土过火砖（俗称“疙瘩砖”）在五大道民居中运用广泛，其厚重的质感和沉稳的色彩，成为天津建筑的标志。其他如清水砖、粗面石材、仿石水刷石、水泥拉毛墙、细卵石墙等材料也很常见，材料的质感与美感体现了天津建筑的纯朴与厚重。建造技术融会了中国南北、世界东西的技术，形成了天津的特色建造技术。如广东会馆戏楼独特而适用的鸡笼斗拱、石家大院的地下通道式的土空调等都为创新之举。

（六）人文资源丰厚

由于天津毗邻北京，开放较早，经济繁荣，社会各界名流涌居天津，天津为他们提供了施展才华的舞台，近代中国上演的历史活剧给天津留下了珍贵的遗迹。经考证，近代有200余位名人政要曾在天津留下了寓所、足迹和故事：革命先驱孙中山、周恩来、邓颖超、张太雷等在此留下了革命斗争的历史；爱国将领张学良、吉鸿昌、张自忠曾将这里作为人生的重要舞台；中国近代史上一批杰出的文教科技界人士梁启超、李叔同、严复、张伯苓、侯德榜等在此创办新学、宣传新文化、实践科技救国的史迹；末代皇帝溥仪、庆亲王载振在这里做过复辟清王朝的白日梦；北洋政府五位大总统袁世凯、徐世昌、黎元洪、冯国璋、曹锟及数任总理和国务大臣在天津上演了一幕幕政治活剧。

伴随这些历史人物，在天津的历史风貌建筑里发生了很多中国近代史的开创性历史事件。曾有学者做过统计，近代中国历史上有130余项“第一”在天津诞生，如第一枚邮票、第一张报纸、第一所现代大学等。这些都构成了天津丰富独特的城市人文和旅游资源。

自《条例》颁布以来，在国家相关法律法规指导下，天津采取了一系列有效的保护措施，持续对历史风貌建筑和街区开展保护工作。在市委市政府正确领导下，市住建委、市规划资源局、市文旅局等部门和相关区政府协同合作，经过十余年的保护实践，在保护理念、法律法规、技术支撑、价值评估、项目整理等5个方面进行了有效探索，逐渐形成了特色的保护体系。天津市先后对877 幢建筑建立了基本档案和安全档案；整修了部分建筑，排除了安全隐患，恢复了建筑的历史风貌，并将部分历史风貌建筑作为展览馆类和文商类建筑对外开放，实现了合理利用。

党的二十大报告强调“加大文物和文化遗产保护力度，加强城乡建设中历史文化保护传承，建好用好国家文化公园”，这为天津历史风貌建筑等文化遗产的保护工作指明了方向。我们将进一步集国内外建筑遗产保护利用经验之长，深入思考保护方向，继续加大保护力度，汇集政府、企业、专家、公众等多方力量，共同守住天津的文化根脉，为“美丽天津”建设注入重要的历史文化元素；致力于让历史风貌建筑在当今社会“活”起来，使其价值惠及当今社会，惠及广大百姓。

疙瘩砖细部
Details of bricks with coarse and lump surface

细卵石墙面
Pea pebble wall

南开学校
Nankai High School

北洋大学
Peiyang University

A SUMMARY OF THE HISTORIC ARCHITECTURE IN TIANJIN

Tianjin Professional Consulting Committee for the Protection of Historic Architecture
Lu Hong[1]

1. General Description

According to the *Protective Regulations on the Tianjin City Historic and Stylistic Architecture (Regulations)* , historic and stylistic architecture is a term referring to any constructions and buildings that have been built for more than 50 years, bearing some architectural features or scientific values in terms of their styles, structures, technical skills, or engineering technologies; reflect the city's historical and cultural or traditional folkway and customs being times or local characteristics; or have present distinguished architectural styles of foreign countries; or refer to the representative construction product of any well-known architects; or have special significance in the revolutionary history; or are those representative workshops, business shops, factories and warehouses in the development of the industry; or are the residences of celebrities as well as other constructions of special historical significance. Those streets or districts where such historic constructions are densely built are called historic and stylistic constructions communities or quarters.

The *Regulations* came into force on the first of September, 2005. According to it, and after the authentication of Tianjin Professional Consulting Committee for the Protection of Historic Architecture, the government confirmed 877 historic constructions in six groups, totaling an area of 1,260,000 m^2. during the period from 2005 to 2013. Of them, 69 buildings are classified as special important ones to be protected, 205 as key ones and 603 as general ones, all distributed across the 15 districts and counties of the city. Of the 877 buildings, there are some relic units of different levels.

Tianjin was confirmed as the national-level historic and cultural city in 1986. In March 2006, the State Council approved the city's overall program including the famous historic and cultural city program, in whilh 14 historic and cultural landscape protective areas were confirmed, and the majority of the historic and stylistic buildings are situated within these protective areas of historic and cultural heritage.

The existing historic constructions include either those quadrangle compounds, guildhalls and temples, all of traditional Chinese styles, or Western classic and modern architecture. Together with those historical and cultural landscape areas, they have formed a unique architectural culture and city spectacle, thus making up the important part of Tianjin City, a national famous historic and cultural city in China.

2. Historical Background

The historic and stylistic constructions and such quarters witnessed the development of the city itself and the society. The earliest relics of human existence left over by our forefathers in the Tianjin area can date back to 10,000 years ago during the Old Stone Age. During the Sui and Tang, or Song and Liao Dynasties, larger groups of human Settlements and constructions appeared in this area. So far, the earliest construction in ancient times we have found is the Dule Temple, which was reconstructed in the second year of the Tonghe period of the reign of Emperor Shengzong of Liao Dynasty (984). In the second year of the Yongle period of the reign of the Ming Emperor Chengzu (1404), a guard was established, called "Tianjin", a name given by Emperor Chengzu (Zhu Di) himself to mark his expedition to the south to seize the state power. Tianjin means the ferry, specially for the emperor. Since then, the history of the city has begun.

Through the Ming and Qing Dynasties, Tianjin took the seat of the old town as its base for construction. Depending on the Canal Culture, the town developed itself from a guard to a sub-prefecture, and then prefecture, or from a simple military guard post to an important township of business and culture in the north China, with businessmen bustling about at that time. The old town was a rectangle in shape, covering an area of about 1.76 km^2, similar to the old towns in ancient China. It was centered on the Drum Tower; streets were laid out in the shape of a cross; along each of the four streets, small lanes or alleys were formed. Except a few constructions of governmental offices or temples of Confucius, which were usually of traditional grandeur structure, the residences of common people were mostly small houses, mixed up partly with the southern-style dwelling houses, presenting a combined style of the traditional houses in the south and the north.

After the Second Opium War in 1860, Tianjin was forced to lend its port to foreign powers. In 1900, the Eight-Power Allied Forces encroached on Tianjin. The old city was destroyed by the forces on November 26 of the same year. Four sections of the city wall were demolished and turned to be four avenues. Since 1860, nine imperialist countries including Britain, France, the United States, Germany, Japan, Russia, Italy, Belgium, and Austria-Hungary acquired the right to supposedly lease a tract of land as concessions in the city one after another. The concessions were formed through three stages.

The first stage: The city ceded tracts of land for concessions to Britain, France and the United States. In 1860, the British-French Allied Forces waged the Second Opium War against China and forced the Chinese Government to sign the *Sino-British Treaty of Beijing* and the *Sino-French Treaty of Beijing* respectively. Tianjin was lent to them to be a port for trade. On December 7th that year, a part of the area on the west bank of the Haihe River including the Purple Bamboo Grove and Xia Yuan Garden was ceded to Britain as its concession in the city. In June, the following year, France and the United States had their concessions on the south and north sides of the area of the British concessions respectively.

The second stage: Germany and Japan seized their concessions and the British concession was expanded. First, Germany acquired its concession on the west bank of the Haihe River in 1895. Then in 1896, Japan had its concession on the west of the French concession. In 1897, Britain arbitrarily expanded the area of its former concession to the north side of the Nanjing Road.

The third stage: The formation of the concessions of the nine countries. In 1900, when the Eight-Power Allied Forces encroached on China, Russia got its concession on the east bank of the Haihe River in 1900, on the south side of which, Belgium seized the area as its concession in 1902. In the same year, Italy had its concession on the north side of the Russia's concession. On the north side of the Italy's concession, a part of the area was seized by Austria-Hungary as its concession. At the same time, Britain, France, Japan and Germany seized the opportunity to expand the area of their concessions. Eventually, all the concessions were concentrated on the both sides of the Haihe River, covering 23,350.5 mu of land (about 1,556.7 hectares). At that time, the seat of the old city only occupied 2,940 mu of land (about 196 hectares), equall to one-eighths of the total area of the concessions.

British concession had been maintained for 85 years—the longest period of all. The Austria-Hungary's concession lasted only 17 years—the shortest. This phenomenon in the history of world's cities has never seen before. Accordingly, Tianjin has suffered the galling shame and humiliation in the modern history of China. Meanwhile, the historic and stylistic constructions together with their multi-culture derived from therein, have become important historic context and valuable cultural resources that cannot be neglected in the city construction. The mushrooming of constructions in the area of concessions brought western architectural culture and technologies into Tianjin as torrents. Architecture of the city developed from its traditional Chinese style to the combination of the Chinese and western styles, triggering off a thriving development of all kinds of styles and fashions in the construction industry.

In the history of Chinese cities, a city that has a history of more than 600 years is still regarded as a young city. As a national famous historic city, Tianjin, though neither having the prominent position in history of such antique capitals as Beijing, Xi'an and Nanjing, nor the brilliant culture as the cities of Yangzhou, Suzhou, and Kaifeng, boasts its own value in terms of the river-sea culture developed by the Grand Canal in the Ming and Qing Dynasties and cultural interchanges between itself and the western countries over the past hundred years. After the Opium War, some of the vestiges of almost all the historical significant events in China can be found in the city. So, in the Chinese historical circles, a prevalent saying goes: "Xi'an is a witness of the past five thousand years, and Beijing, a witness of the past 1,000 years, while Tianjin, a witness of the past 100 years."

3. Types of Constructions

The numerous historic constructions in Tianjin have lasted for more than 1,000 years, including dwelling houses, public constructions and warehouse. For convenient management and study, they can be classified into three categories.

1) Constructions Built in Chronological Order

After the Second Opium War in 1860, Tianjin was forced to lend its port to foreign countries and gradually to cede its tracts of land to nine imperialist countries as concessions, and the construction in the city developed itself from the traditional Chinese style to a combination of the Chinese and Western styles, marking a great change of times and the ideas with a distinctive symbol. Therefore, taking the year 1860 as the watershed, we can classify the historic constructions as the ancient ones (before 1860) and the modern ones (after 1860).

The ancient ones mainly include traditional Chinese-style architecture. So far, only about 50 such constructions have been left over, most of which are distributed in Jizhou, and the seat of the old city, such as the Dule Temple of Liao Dynasty (built in 984), the Temple for Queen of Heaven of Yuan Dynasty (built in 1326) and the Taoist Temple of Jade Emperor of Ming Dynasty (built in 1427).

The modern ones are treasures of the city with the largest quantity and the most distinctive characteristics, mainly distributed on the both sides of the Haihe River in the downtown of the city.

2) Constructions Classified into Ten Categories by Functions

Dwelling houses are the most in quantity, with most distinctive characteristics. Of these houses, some can be further classified as separated courtyard or compound mansions, flat or apartment and apartment in a block. Other types include school constructions, banking constructions, business and trading headquarters, office buildings, factories and warehouses, churches, entertainment and sports facilities, hospitals, communication facilities.

3) Constructions Classified into Five Categories by Exterior Features

Traditional Chinese bureaucratic constructions: They were built strictly in accordance with the traditional type and system of the officialdom, mainly including temples, government offices, such as the Temple for Queen of Heaven, Taoist Temple and of Jade Emperor, Compound of Great Mercy.

European classic renaissance styled constructions: Most of such constructions were modeled after the constructions of ancient Greece and Rome and those were built during the period of Renaissance, such as the office building of Kailuan Mining Administration , Former Hongkong and Shanghai Bank Corporation.

Eclectic styled constructions: These are combinations of buildings modeling on typical European classic styles and the eclectic patterns together with both the Chinese and western styles. Most constructions in the city can be grouped into this category, such as the former residences of Bao Guiqing.

Dwelling houses of common people: They include traditional Chinese styled common houses and the local courtyard-styled compounds such as Shi's Family compound, and Xu's Family compound. Many other living houses were modeled after the typical European-styled houses such as the Spanish-styled, British-styled, German-styled and Italian-styles houses.

Modern houses: These constructions were built with new materials and in new structures, such as Leopold Building and Bohai Building.

4. Basic Characteristics

1) Constructions being built in a comparatively concentrated period of time. About 60 percent of all the historic constructions were built during the period from 1900 to 1937, less than a period of 40 years.

2) Constructions of each type being built in a concentrated area, making up a quarter of buildings. Traditional Chinese style constructions were concentrated on the seat of the old city and in the Ancient Culture Street. Banking buildings were mainly densely built in the North Jiefang Road, known as "Financial Avenue". Business and trading buildings were concentrated in the Heping Road and the Gu Yi Street and the Ancient Culture Street. Common dwelling houses were on

the seat of the old city, the Yigong Garden of the Hebei District, Dayingmen of the Hexi District, the Fifth Avenue of the Heping District and near the Central Garden. Warehouses were mostly built along the banks of the Haihe River.

3) The modern designs and techniques of historic constructions following the patterns of constructions in Western countries, such as the followings.

— Advanced ideas of design: During the 1920s, when the new idea of building a "gardening city" was prevalent in Britain, constructions being built in the new district of the British concession (now the Five Avenues district) at that time were mostly following the practice of this idea. The scope of the residential quarter was moderate, and the quarter was equipped with such facilities as schools, churches and playgrounds, providing a pleasant and comfortable living environment. New model of apartments and flats in a block was also introduced from their origin to Tianjin.

— Complete public support facilities and interior room equipment: All the concessions paid attention to the leveling of ground and construction of roads and perfection of municipal engineering and facilities, such as road lamps, treeplanting, and providing utilities, and flush toilets, so as to improve the living environment and hygienic conditions.

— Advanced idea of development of real estate and property industry: All the concessions introduced the Western idea and patterns in the development of real estate and property, for instance, the British and French concessions divided a tract of land into squares, encircled on four sides by roads, to lend them out at different times.

— Modern way of life and the different city activities: The Western way of life in modern times was introduced into the concessions when they were being built. For instance, the family way of life centered on a living room, a dining room or a ballroom; the public way of life took parks, churches, and the town council as its center of activities; and the people's walking on foot was replaced usually by modern traffic means of trams or automobiles. This modern way of life was quite different from the conservative way of life long time maintained by Chinese people and it also brought in diversified activities in the city.

4) A diversity of construction styles and arts: Influenced by both the traditional Chinese and Western architectural trends of thought, a co-existence situation had been created of the traditional Chinese style, classic renaissance style, eclectic style and modern style. They added radiation and beauty to each other, together presenting a unique and rich city spectacle of Tianjin.

5) Outstanding features of construction materials and techniques: The unique construction materials and techniques must owe to the city's unique geographical environment and its water and soil. These materials and techniques were fully brought into the constructions. For instance, the chamottoe bricks (or known as bricks with coarse gravels on the surface) were widely used in the common houses in the Five Avenues, becoming a special mark of Tianjin's constructions with their solid quality and grave colors. Other materials like fair-faced bricks, coarse-surfaced slabs, imitation water dressing stones, stucco plastered bricks walls and pea pebbles wall were also used. The constructions introduced techniques from the south and north of China, and the east and west of the world to create the city's unique techniques. For example, the chicken coop-shaped dougong, a traditional Chinese construction technique, was used in the theater stage of Guangdong Guildhall and the self-built underground tunnel conditioner in the Shi's Family compound were all newly created.

6) Affluent humanity resources: Because Tianjin is close to Beijing, and was opened earlier to the outside world, a number of celebrities of society swarmed into the city, where they had opportunities to develop their capabilities and talents. The historical drama staged in modern China has left over precious legacy to the city. According to textual research, about 200 dignified personalities have left over to the city their residences, "footprints" and anecdotes. The revolutionary pioneers like Dr. Sun Yat-sen, Zhou Enlai, Deng Yingchao and Zhang Tailei had led the revolutionary activities in the city; Patriotic generals like Zhang Xueliang, Ji Hongchang, Zhang Zizhong, had regarded Tianjin as a important stage of their lives; scientists and scholars like Liang Qichao, Li Shutong, Yan Fu, Zhang Boling, and Hou Debang, had devoted themselves to the introduction of modern schools, publicity of new cultures, and the practice of salvation of the country by science and technology; Pu Yi, the last emperor of the Qing Dynasty, and Zai Zhen, the imperial prince Qing, had their daydreams of restoration of a dethroned monarch; The five presidents of the Northern Warlord Government (Beiyang Government) Yuan Shikai, Xu Shichang, Li Yuanhong, Feng Guozhang, and Cao Kun and its premiers and ministers of different tenures of office had staged a political farce in the city.

Along with all these historical figures, a number of events of pioneering significance had occurred in these constructions in the modern history of China. According to statistics made by a scholar, about 130 items of inventions originated in the city, including the first postage stamp, the first newspaper, and the first university. They have constituted a part of the city's humanity and tourism resources.

Since the promulgation of the regulations, under the guidance of relevant laws and regulations, Tianjin has adopted a series of effective protection measures to protect historic buildings and blocks continuously. Under the correct leadership of the municipal committee and the municipal government, the municipal housing and Construction Commission, the municipal Planning and Resources Bureau, the municipal cultural and Tourism Bureau, and other departments and the relevant district governments have cooperated, and after more than ten years of protection practice, in the concept of protection, laws and regulations, technical support, value assessment, project sorted out five aspects of effective exploration, and gradually formed a feature of the protection system. The basic archives and safety archives of 877 buildings have been established successively; some buildings have been renovated, hidden safety hazards have been eliminated, and the historical features of the buildings have been restored, some of the historic buildings are opened to the public as exhibition halls and commercial buildings, which can be used reasonably.

The 20th National Congress report stressed that"put more effort into protecting cultural artifacts and heritage, better protect and preserve historical and cultural heritage in the course of urban and rural development, and build and make good use of national cultural parks.", which has pointed out the direction for the protection of Tianjin's cultural heritage, such as historical buildings. We will further pool our experience in the conservation and utilization of architectural heritage at home and abroad, think deeply about the direction of conservation, continue to step up conservation efforts, bring together the government, enterprises, experts, the public and other forces to work together to preserve the cultural roots of Tianjin and inject important historical and cultural elements into the construction of a"Beautiful Tianjin." We will work hard to make historic buildings"Live" in today's society so that their values will benefit today's society and the general public.

外景 Exterior view

山门 Entrance Hall

独乐寺
Dule Temple

独乐寺坐落于蓟州区武定街41号，全国重点文物保护单位，特殊保护等级历史风貌建筑，占地面积约16 500 m^2，建筑面积约1 600 m^2。相传其始建于唐朝初年，山门和观音阁于辽统和二年（984年）重建，是中国现存最古老的楼阁式木结构建筑。独乐寺由山门、观音阁、东西配殿、乾隆皇帝行宫、卧佛殿、三世佛宝殿、文物陈列室、僧房等建筑组成。山门庑殿顶之鸱吻为中国现存较早的鸱吻造型；柱框和上层屋架之间的斗拱是中国木结构建筑现存较早的斗拱实例；观音阁内供奉的观音像高16 m，有十一个头像，也称“十一面观音”，是中国现存最大的泥塑佛像之一。“独乐寺”匾额出自明代严嵩手笔。

Dule Temple is located at 41 Wuding Street, Jizhou District of Tianjin, covering an area of about 16,500 square meters, and about 1,600 square meters in floor space. Known as the important heritage site under state protection and the special protection historic architecture in Tianjin, the Dule Temple was initially built in the early Tang Dynasty, as one of the most ancient wooden pavilion-styled relics in China. And its Entrance Hall and Guanyin Pavilion were rebuilt in 984, the second year of the Tonghe's Reign, Liao Dynasty.

As one of the most ancient wooden pavilion-styled relics in China, Dule Temple is a building complex including the Entrance Hall, Guanyin Pavilion, East & West Side Halls, Royal Hall for Emperor Qianlong, Sleeping-Buddha Hall, Buddhas of the Middle, East and West, Showroom and monk's dormitory, etc. The Chiwen-shaped ornaments on the ridges of the Entrance Hall have been considered to be in older Chiwen style preserved in China. And the brackets between columns and roof trusses are also realized as the older ones preserved well among the ancient wooden structures in China.

The Bodhisattva statue in Guanyin Pavilion is 16m high with 11 faces, which could be considered as one of the biggest clay Buddha sculptures preserved in China. The inscriptions on the horizontal tablet of the Dule Temple was the handwritings of Yansong (1480-1567), the premier of Ming Dynasty.

观音阁 Guanyin Pavilion

琳宇近神畿慈雲廣蔭

十一面观音菩萨塑像
Statue of the 11-faced Guanyin Bodhisattva

观音阁顶层木结构
Wooden structure inside the top layer of the Guanyin Pavilion

观音阁内塑像
Statue in the Guanyin Pavilion

外檐局部
Partial outer-eaves

外檐局部
Partial outer-eaves

观音阁壁画
Mural paintings in the Guanyin Pavilion

外景 Exterior view

玉皇阁
Taoist Temple of Jade Emperor

玉皇阁位于南开区古文化街，天津市文物保护单位，特殊保护等级历史风貌建筑。其建于明初，明宣德二年（1427年）重建，是天津市区内现存最大的道观。因其地势较高，濒临老三岔河口，视野开阔，明清两代每年农历正月初八在这里举行"祭星"，重阳节举行登高、"攒斗"等活动。现仅存的主体建筑清虚阁，为砖木结构二层楼阁式建筑，重檐歇山屋顶，屋面采用黄琉璃绿剪边做法，是典型的中国传统大式建筑。

Known as the heritage site under city protection and the special protection historic architecture in Tianjin, Taoist Temple of Jade Emperor erects in the Ancient Cultural Street, Nankai District of Tianjin. It was originally constructed in the early stage of Ming Dynasty, and re-constructed in 1427, the second year of the Xuande's Reign. It is the biggest preserved Taoist temple in the downtown.

The temple stands on a high site nearby the joint of 3 rivers, with a bird's eye view of the land below. Therefore, it has served as the Taoist altar to offer sacrifices to Star Gods and Goddesses on the 8th day of Chinese Lunar January and to congratulate the Mother of Star Gods on her birthday on the 9th day of Chinese lunar calendar September each year.

Qingxu Pavilion is the only building preserved among the main ones of the temple. Such a two-layer structure is made of wood and bricks, showing its features typically as the grand Chinese architecture: double-eave gable-hip roofs covered by the yellow glazed tiles and bordered by green glazed tiles.

雪景 Snow view

外景 Exterior view

二层阁楼 Top attic of the Qingxu Pavilion

歇山屋顶 Gable-and-hip roofs

外景 Exterior view

天后宫

Temple for Queen of Heaven

天后宫位于南开区古文化街80号，全国重点文物保护单位，特殊保护等级历史风貌建筑，初建于元泰定三年（1326年），原名“天妃宫”，俗称“娘娘宫”，历经多次重修，是天津市区最古老的建筑群，也是中国现存年代最早的妈祖庙之一。每年天后诞辰，以天后宫为中心会举行大型民间酬神庙会活动，沿河船户、周边信众亦纷纷到来，各地商贾云集，造就了天津最著名的商业街——宫南宫北大街（今古文化街）的繁荣。该建筑群坐西朝东，面向海河，由山门、牌坊、前殿、大殿等组成，属典型的中国传统庙宇式建筑。

Temple for Queen of Heaven, also called Tian-hou-gong Taoist Temple popularly, sits at No.80 Ancient Cultural Street, Nankai District. As the important heritage site under state protection and the special protection historic architecture in Tianjin, the temple was originally built in 1326, the third year of Taiding's Reign, Yuan Dynasty and has been restored for seneral times since then. Being one of the earliest Matzu temples in China, it is considered as the most ancient building complex in the city centre.

Every year while the Queen's birthday is coming, series of the spectacular cultural and folk missions are being launched around the temple for offering sacrifices to Gods and Goddesses. And the merchants also take the opportunities to gather here from anywhere for their business, thus making the street nearby become a famous commercial center, which has been opened as the Ancient Cultural Street nowadays.

Looking down to the Haihe River, the temple faces eastward and mainly consists of the Entrance Hall, Gateway, Front Hall and Grand Hall (Main Hall). It is characterized as the typical Chinese temple architecture.

前殿正面 Facade of the Front Hall

外景 Exterior view

内院回廊 Cloister

清真大寺

Great Mosque

清真大寺位于红桥区小伙巷清真大寺前街8号，天津市文物保护单位，特殊保护等级历史风貌建筑。清真大寺始建于清顺治元年（1644年），为穆斯林群众礼拜和集会的场所。历经康熙十八年（1679年）、嘉庆六年（1801年）、咸丰二年（1852年）、光绪三十一年（1905年）的多次续建，以至现在的规模，建筑面积约1 800 m^2，均为砖木结构，灰瓦坡顶，青砖墙面。该建筑群以大殿为主体，另设对厅、讲堂、耳房、沐浴室等，布局紧凑。大殿（礼拜殿）由四组单体歇山顶建筑组成，分前后殿，高大宽敞，其他附属用房为硬山屋顶。整个建筑群均采用中国传统建筑风格。

Located at No.8 Great Mosque Front Street, Xiaohuo Lane, Hongqiao District, Tianjin, the Great Mosque is the heritage site under city protection and the special protection historic architecture in Tianjin. Established in 1644 (the first year of Shunzhi's Reign, Qing Dynasty), the mosque is a place for Muslims to gather and worship. Being renovated and expanded in 1679 (the eighteenth year of Kangxi's Reign, Qing Dynasty), 1801 (the sixth year reign of Jiaqing Emperor of Qing Dynasty), 1852 (the second year of Xianfeng's Reign, Qing Dynasty) and 1905 (the thirty-first year of Guangxu's Reign, Qing Dynasty), the mosque finally reached the current scale and has a floor area of 1,800 square meters. The mosque is a brick-wood structure with sloping roof covered by grey tiles and walls made of grey bricks. The complex is a compact whole and includes the main hall, lecture hall, auxiliary rooms, bathroom, etc. The main hall (worshiping hall) is covered with four gable and rip roofs and divided into front and back halls. The other rooms are covered with Chinese gabled roofs. The whole complex follows traditional Chinese architectural style.

大殿内景
View inside the main hall

大殿外景 Exterior view of the main hall

帝德清淨無爲遵王道之蕩蕩平平億萬人
胥歸化育

雪景 Snow view

西开教堂
Xikai Catholic Church

西开教堂位于和平区西宁道11号，天津市文物保护单位，特殊保护等级历史风貌建筑。建于1916年，初名为“圣约瑟堂”，因地处老西开，也叫“西开教堂”。教堂建成后，法租界当局以保护教堂为借口，向老西开扩展租界，引发了“老西开事件”。该建筑平面呈拉丁十字形构图，建筑面积约2 000 m^2，高42 m，两侧巨型穹顶内为木结构支撑，外包铜片；外墙面采用红、黄色砖相间清水砌筑，檐口下采用扶壁连列柱券作装饰带；立面以圆形窗和列柱券形窗组成的半圆形叠砌拱窗为要素，为华北地区最大的罗马风格教堂建筑。

The Xikai Catholic Church is located at No.11 Xining Avenue, Heping District, being the heritage site under city protection and the special protection historic architecture in Tianjin.

The Xikai Catholic Church, originally called Church of St. Joseph, was set up in 1916. It is more popularly known as the Xikai Catholic Church, for it sits in the Old Xikai Area. Soon after the foundation of the church, the authorities of the French Concession tried to extend their territory into the Old Xikai Area under the plea to keep safe of the church. The action was certainly fought back by the Chinese people at once, which is the “Lao Xikai Event”.

The church was designed in a Latin cross plan, 42 meters in height, and about 2,000 square meters in floor area. The timberwork bearings coated with copper sheets were adopted to support the two massive domes at both sides. The dry walls were made up with red and yellow bricks in alternate order. The cornices were decorated by buttress combined with columned arch-windows . It serves as the biggest Roman Church in North China.

外檐局部
Partial outer-eaves

外景 Exterior view

鸟瞰图
Bird's eye view

内景 Inner view

外檐局部 Partial outer-eaves

望海楼教堂
Wanghailou Catholic Church

望海楼教堂位于河北区狮子林大街292号，全国重点文物保护单位，特殊保护等级历史风貌建筑，始建于1869年，系法国天主教会修建，初名为“圣母得胜堂”，俗称“望海楼教堂”。在1870年“天津教案”运动和1900年“义和团”运动中，先后两次被焚毁，又两次重建。现存教堂系1904年法国教会利用庚子赔款在原址重建，建筑面积约1 900 m^2。该建筑为砖木结构二层楼房，正中高耸塔楼，两侧建有角楼。建筑立面处理精巧别致，细部丰富，具有哥特式建筑特征。

Known as the important heritage site under state protection and the special protection historic architecture in Tianjin, the Wanghailou Catholic Church is located at No.292 Shizilin Street, Hebei District, covering an area of about 1,900 square meters in floor space.

The church was built in 1869 by the missions of the French Catholic Church and was named Notre Dame des Victories (Church of St. Victorious Victory). It had been burned down because of the Tianjin Missionary Case and Boxer Uprising respectively in 1870 and 1900, and rebuilt twice afterwards.

The preserved church was rebuilt in 1904 by the French Church with the Boxer Indemnity. The brick-wood structure is two-storied, with two turrets on both sides and a highly erected tower in between. It is typically characterized as a Gothic design considering its elegant elevation treatments and abundant details.

外檐局部 Partial outer-eaves

夜景 Night view

内景 Inner view

外景 Exterior view

安里甘教堂
All Saints' Anglican Church

安里甘教堂位于和平区浙江路2号，天津市文物保护单位，重点保护等级历史风貌建筑。安里甘教堂也称“安里甘教会诸圣堂”，1903年建成，由英租界工部局筹建，属圣公会系统，受英国国外布道会及圣公会华北教区管辖，是天津英国基督教安里甘教派信徒礼拜之所。该建筑1935年毁于火灾，1936年复建，为砖木结构平房，设有地下室、钟楼，多坡屋顶牛舌瓦屋面，屋顶中部设有尖顶塔楼；建筑平面布局为集中式，室内空间开敞，装饰简洁大气；外檐为青砖清水墙面，墙面以联排券柱和砖雕花饰作装饰带，门、窗均有多重砖券，朴素又不失典雅，具有哥特式建筑特征。

Standing at No.2 Zhejiang Road, Heping District, Tianjin, the Episcopal Church is the heritage site under city protection and the important protection historic architecture in Tianjin. Also known as All Saints' Anglican Church, the church was established in 1903 by the British Concession Municipal Committee. As a member of All Aaints' Church and under the jurisdiction of British Evangelical Overseas Outreach and North China Parish of All Saints' Church, the church is a place for British Anglican Christians to worship the God. The building was burnt down in 1935 and was rebuilt in 1936. As a brick-wood structure, the church has basement, bell tower, and is covered with sloping roofs. The middle part of the roof has a steeple tower. The rooms in the building are spacious and elegantly decorated. Dry walls of grey bricks form the exterior of the building are decorated with rows of arched columns and brick carvings. The doors and windows of the building are arched with layers of bricks, giving it a humble and elegant look. It epitomizes the Gothic architectural style.

内檐局部
Partial inner-eaves

外景 Exterior view

伯苓楼门廊 Entrance Portico of the Boling Building

南开学校
Nankai High School

南开学校位于南开区南开四马路20~22号，全国重点文物保护单位，现存南楼、东楼、北楼、瑞庭礼堂等四幢特殊保护等级历史风貌建筑。南开学校始建于清光绪三十年（1904年），是天津最早的私立中学。创办人为著名教育家严修、张伯苓。初名“私立中学堂”，旋改名“私立敬业中学堂”，清光绪三十一年（1905年）改称“私立第一中学堂”。清光绪三十三年（1907年）建成新校舍，改称“私立南开中学堂”。中华人民共和国成立后改为“公立中学”，1960年恢复“南开中学”校名。1913—1917年，周恩来总理曾在此就读；1954—1960年，温家宝总理曾在此就读。

东楼、北楼为砖木结构二层楼房，坡屋顶，青砖饰面。建筑首层开方窗，二层为连续拱券窗，拱券门洞突出入口，造型别致。建筑形体简单，但细部处理繁复。东楼（现伯苓楼）建于1906年，为当时南开学校的中心建筑；北楼建于1913年；南楼亦称“范孙楼”，建于1929年，阎子亨设计，是为纪念严修先生由张伯苓倡议、海内外校友捐建的，砖混结构三层楼房（设有地下室），局部四层，既体现了中式建筑特色，又吸取了欧洲古典建筑手法；瑞庭礼堂建于1934年，砖木结构，外檐为青砖清水墙面，能容纳1 700人。

The Nankai High School stands at No.20-22 Fourth Nankai Road, Nankai District. 4 well-preserved buildings of the school have been listed as the important heritage site under state protection and the special protection historic architecture in Tianjin. As the earliest private secondary school in Tianjin, the Private Nankai Middle School was founded in 1904(the 30th year of Guangxu's Reign, Qing Dynasty) by Yan Xiu and Zhang Boling, very famous educationists in China. Soon after, it had its name changed

伯苓楼侧立面
Side view of the Boling Building

範孫樓

into the Private Jingye (Diligence) Middle School and then the Private first Middle School the next year in 1905. Private Nankai High School, a new name was adopted for the school when it moved to its new site completed in 1907. It was once reformed as a public school while the PRC established, but got it name back in 1960 as Nankai High School. Premier Zhou Enlai studied here in 1913–1917, and Premier Wen Jiabao studied here in 1954–1960.

Both of its East and North Buildings are two- storied with brick-wood structure. The sloping-roofed buildings have got their walls black-brick finished with the windows in square shape at the first layer but arch shape opened one by one at the second. Accompanied by the elegant arched gateways standing against the entrances, the buildings look simple in style but complex in details. The East building (Boling Building)was set up in 1906 as the central architecture in the school, and the North one built in 1931. Known as the Fansun Building, the South Building was constructed in 1929 sponsored financially by the graduates of the school at home and abroad. Having adopted the propose of Mr. Zhang Boling, the building was named after Mr. Yan Xiu (alias Yan Fansun) in memory of him. Built in 1934, the Ruiting Auditorium was of brick-wood structure with 1,700 seats.

范孙楼外景 View of the Fansun Building

伯苓楼外景
Exterior view of the Boling Building

天津南

礼堂外景
Exterior view of the Ruiting Auditorium

原天津公学

Former Tianjin College

原天津公学位于和平区南京路106号，天津市文物保护单位，特殊保护等级历史风貌建筑。原天津公学始建于1927年，为天津租界中第一所华人学校。天津租界内的学校为外侨子女专有，不允许华人子弟入学。租界内的中国人为争取子女受教育的权利，由天津实业家、英租界工部局华人董事庄乐峰主持向英租界当局申办，并倡议捐资筹建此校。当时校址初设英租界戈登道（今湖北路），1929年迁至现址。1935年改名为“耀华学校”，取“光耀中华”之意。现名为“耀华中学”。

该校现存历史风貌建筑五幢，建筑面积约11 000 m^2，由英商永固工程司设计。建筑外檐均为红砖清水墙面，每幢建筑入口均建有简化的混水饰面的罗马柱式或山花，与清水红砖墙形成鲜明对比，整组建筑具有折中主义特征。

Located at No.106 Nanjing Road, Heping District, Tianjin, the former Tianjin College is the heritage site under city protection and the special protection historic architecture in Tianjin. Constructed in 1927, the school was the first Chinese school established in the concession area of Tianjin. Schools in the concession area were open only to children of foreign employees working in China but children of Chinese citizens were not allowed in these schools. To fight for the education right of Chinese children, Zhuang Lefeng, an industrialist and the president of municipal committee of the British concession, applied for and advocated the establishment of this school with donated fund on behalf of all Chinese citizens living in the concession. The location of the school was previously in Gedeng Avenue (now Hubei Road) of British concession. In 1929, the school was moved to the current location. In 1935, it was renamed as Yaohua School, suggesting that it should bring glory to China. It is called Yaohua Middle School now.

Having a floor area of 11,000 square meters, the school is home to five historic buildings, all designed by the British Eversolid Engineering Company. Dry walls constructed with red bricks form the exterior of the buildings. Decorated and plastered Rome columns can be found at each entrance of the buildings, a sharp contrast to the red fair-faced walls. The whole complex has the characteristics of eclecticism architecture.

外檐门
Gate under the outer-eaves

外景 Exterior view

外景 Exterior view

原英国公学

Former British College

原英国公学位于和平区湖北路59号，全国重点文物保护单位，重点保护等级历史风貌建筑，现为二十中学。始建于1905年，为英侨子弟学校，由在津英侨捐办，1928年迁入现址，学校当时对一切外国侨民开放。著名记者伊斯雷尔·爱泼斯坦即毕业于该校。该建筑建成于1928年，建筑面积约6 000 m²，由英商永固工程司库克和安德森设计，砖木结构二层楼房，局部三层，设有地下室，平面布局对称，呈飞机形。教室设置于一、二层的“机翼”部位，主入口设于“机头”部位；外檐为红瓦坡顶，混水墙面。开放的入口门廊和高耸的屋顶对应，使建筑虚实变化强烈，气势恢弘，具有仿希腊古典复兴建筑风格。

Located at No.59 Hubei Road, Heping District, Tianjin, the former British College is the important heritage site under state protection and the important protection historic architecture in Tianjin. It is now the Twentieth Middle School. Established in 1905 as a school for children of British employees working in China, the school was founded with money donated by British employees. In 1928, the school moved to the current site and was open to children of all the foreign employees working in Tianjin. Israel Epstein, a well-known journalist, once studied here. Constructed in 1928, the building has a floor area of 6,000 square meters and was designed by Cook & Anderson, two engineers from the British Eversolid Engineering Company. The building is a two-storied brick-wood structure with part of the building having three floors. The building, equipped with a basement, is symmetrically designed and shaped like an plane. The classrooms find their presence at the tail of the plane, on both the first and second floor. The main entrance is at the head of the plane. The building is covered with sloping roof and red tiles and the walls are plastered brick walls. The open porch and the lofty roof give the building a strong contrast and a magnificent touch. It is a copy of the Greek classical architectural style.

一楼大厅内柱廊
Colonnade on the first floor

雪景 Snow view

主楼外檐局部
Partial outer-eaves of the Main building

原天津工商学院

Former Tianjin College of Industry and Commerce

原天津工商学院建成于1925年，位于河西区马场道117~119号。中华人民共和国成立后，工学院并入天津大学，商学院并入南开大学，师范学院扩建为天津师范学院。1970年原址改为天津外国语学院。现院内存有历史风貌建筑6幢。其中主楼建于1925年，建筑面积约5 600 m^2，全国重点文物保护单位，特殊保护等级历史风貌建筑。该建筑由法商永和工程司设计，为混合结构三层楼房，红瓦坡顶，清水砖墙；建筑平面对称；立面强调古典构图原则，楼顶建有法国曼赛尔结构穹顶；西侧建有内部小教堂，采用半穹顶，独具特色。

The former Tianjin College of Industry and Commerce was founded in 1925, located at No.117~119 Machang Avenue, Hexi District. After the establishmen of the PRC, its Industry and College were merged into Tianjin University and Commerce College into Nankai University, while its Normal College was transferred as the Tianjin Normal College independently.

In 1970, the original site of the former Tianjin College of Industry and Commerce initially served for the Tianjin Foreign Language Institute. There are 6 historic buildings preserved on campus. Among them, the Main Building built in 1925 has been classified as the important heritage site under state protection and the special protection historic architecture in Tianjin, which is about 5,600 square meters in floor space. Designed by the Hunke & Muller, a French business, the composite structure is three-storied with red-tiled sloping roof and dry brick walls. It is a symmetrical design, presenting with Classical taste. A typical French dome is adopted to the roof. A Chapel was designed with a semi-dome on the west side of the building, looking outlandish indeed.

雪景 Snow view

主楼外景
Exterior view of the Main Building

办公楼 Office Building

九楼外景
Exterior view of No.9 Building

天津大学（北洋大学）

Tianjin University (Peiyang University)

天津大学（北洋大学）位于南开区卫津路92号，校内现已确定公布历史风貌建筑四幢，天津市文物保护单位。该校成立于1895年，由原北洋大学与河北工学院合并组成。1952年，全国大学院系调整，天津大学、南开大学、津沽大学合并为两校，天津大学成为以理工为主的大学。校园内四幢历史风貌建筑均为天津大学建筑系建筑师的作品，全部为砖混结构楼房，外檐为硫缸砖清水墙面，在建筑中较多地体现了中国传统文化的元素，其中作为办公楼的九楼尤为突出，毛泽东主席视察天津大学时曾在该楼的台阶上接见该校师生。

Located at No. 92 Weijin Road, Nankai District, Tianjin University (Peiyang University) has four historic buildings and all are the heritage site under city protection. The university was established in 1895, constituted by the amalgamation of original Peiyang University and Hebei University of Technology. In 1952, all the universities in China had undergone a reform of faculties. Tianjin University, Nankai University and Jingu University had been merged into two universities, of which Tianjin University became focused on science and engineering. The four historic buildings on the campus were all the masterpieces of the architects in the department of architecture of the university. They are all reinforced concrete structures with glaze quarry-tiled fair-faced external walls. Traditional Chinese cultural elements can be seen throughout the building with the No. 9 Building which is used as an office building in particular. Chairman Mao Zedong used to meet the teachers and students on the stairs of the building while he was inspecting the university.

九楼外檐局部
Partial outer-eaves of No.9 Building

九楼外景
Exterior view of No.9 Building

八楼外景 Exterior view of No.8 Building

第8教学楼
Building No.8
天津市历史风貌建筑

北楼外景 Exterior view of the North Wing

南楼外景 Exterior view of the South Wing

原北洋大学堂

Former Peiyang University

原北洋大学堂位于红桥区光荣道2号，现存重点保护等级历史风貌建筑三幢，全国重点文物保护单位。北洋大学始建于1895年，是中国第一所现代大学。校址初设梁家园，名“北洋西学学堂”，1902年迁至现址，辛亥革命后改名“北洋大学校”“国立北洋大学”。南楼建于1933年，北楼建于1936年，两幢教学楼均为三层砖混结构楼房，建筑布局对称，体形简洁大方。

The former Peiyang University is located at No.2 Guangrong Avenue, Hongqiao District. 3 well-preserved buildings of the school have been listed as the important heritage site under state protection and the important protection historic architecture in Tianjin. Former Peiyang University, founded in 1895, was the first modern university in China. The original location of the university was in the Liangjiayuan, known as Peiyang West Culture School. In 1902, the school moved to the current location. After the Revolution of 1911, it was renamed Peiyang Grand School and National Peiyang University. The South Wing was constructed in 1933, while the North Wing was constructed in 1936. Both buildings are three-storied brick-concrete in a symmetrical structure. They look simple but elegant.

南楼主入口
Main entrance of the South Wing

外景 Exterior view

B 原开滦矿务局大楼
Building of the Former Kailuan Mining Administration

原开滦矿务局大楼位于和平区泰安道5号，天津市文物保护单位，特殊保护等级历史风貌建筑，现为办公用房，建于1921年，由英商爱迪克生和达拉斯（同和）工程司设计。开滦矿务局的前身为开平矿务局和滦州煤矿。开平矿是晚清官督商办矿，被英商占有。直隶政府建滦州煤矿，企图以滦制开，后竟争失败。1912年两矿合并，成立中英合资的开滦矿务局。其建筑面积约9 000 m^2，混合结构三层楼房（设有地下室），外檐为水刷石断块墙面。建筑采用严格对称的古典三段式构图，正立面设有十四根贯通一、二层的爱奥尼克石柱，造型庄严稳重，简洁大方，属典型的古典主义风格建筑。

The building is located at No.5 Taian Avenue, Heping District, listed as the heritage site under city protection and the special protection historic architecture in Tianjin. The building is used as an office building nowadays and about 9,000 square meters in floor area. It was designed by the English designing body, Atkinson & Dallas Architects and Civil Engineers Ltd. and built in 1921.

The Kailuan Mining Administration was transformed from the Kaiping Colliery combined with Luanzhou Colliery. The Kaiping Colliery was earlier run by the Qing government but occupied by the British late in the Qing Dynasty. The Qing government turned to open another one—Luanzhou Colliery, aiming at competing with the Kaiping Colliery but in failure. And in 1912, the two collieries were incorporated as a Chinese-British joint venture, Kailuan Mining Administration.

The composite structure is three-storied along with its basement and outer-walls faced with granolithic blocks. It is composed classically of three sections in a strictly symmetrical structure. 14 giant Ionic columns along the facade stand erectly up to the height of the second floor. The building looks massive and tasteful, classified as a simple but elegant design in classical style.

一楼大厅大理石台阶
Marble stairs in the lobby of first floor

大厅内景
View inside the lobby

外景 Exterior view

泰安道
7

主入口 Main Entrance

原大清邮政津局

Former Post Office of Qing Dynasty

原大清邮政津局位于和平区解放北路103~111号，天津市文物保护单位，特殊保护等级历史风貌建筑，建于19世纪末，现为办公、居住、商业用房混用，占地面积约1 000 m^2，建筑面积约2 500 m^2。大清邮政津局前身为1878年建成通邮的天津海关书信馆，1897年改为"大清邮政津局"。1878年，该局发行了中国第一套以蟠龙为图案和印有"大清邮政局"字样的1分银、3分银和5分银三种面值的大龙邮票。该建筑为二层砖木结构楼房（设有地下室），青砖墙面，并配有精美砖雕，拱形门窗，体现了欧洲古典主义建筑风格和中国传统砖雕工艺的完美结合。

The Former Post Office of Qing Dynasty is located in No.103~111 North Jiefang Road, Heping District, as the heritage site under city protection and the special protection historic architecture in Tianjin. The building is used for office, dwelling and commercial nowadays, covering an area of about 1,000 square meters, and about 2,500 square meters in floor area. Known as Tianjin Custom Letter House built in 1878, it was renamed Post Office of Qing Tianjin in 1897. The first set of Chinese Dragon Stamps was issued here in 1878, including the versions of one cent, three cent and five cent. This brick-wood two-storied building was constructed in the late 1800s with a flat roof and basement underground. The classicism is emphasized by the delicate carvings on the black bricks on the facade as well as those arched gates and windows. European classicalism and traditional Chinese technique are well combined in this building.

外檐局部
Partial outer-eaves

外景 Exterior view

门廊 Entrance portico

原英国领事官邸

Former British Consul's Mansion

原英国领事官邸位于和平区浙江路1号，天津市文物保护单位，特殊保护等级历史风貌建筑，现为办公用房。英国驻津领事馆设于1860年，1899年升格为总领事馆。该建筑建于1937年，建筑面积约1 700 m^2，砖木结构二层楼房，平面布局不规则，外檐为硫缸砖清水墙面，主入口处由简化的爱奥尼克柱支撑上部露台，建筑转角处均附设壁柱；多坡屋顶，大筒瓦屋面上出老虎窗，檐部出挑，屋顶原有圆形塔楼，1976年地震中震损；室内装饰豪华，木楼梯、木地板、木门窗至今保存完好。建筑整体造型简洁大方，细部装饰精美，具有英国民居风格。

Standing at No.1 Zhejiang Road, Heping District, Tianjin, the former British Consul's Mansion is the heritage site under city protection and the special protection historic architecture in Tianjin and it is now an office building. Established in Tianjin in 1860, the British Consulate was promoted to consulate-general in 1899. The building, completed in 1937, has a floor area of 1,700 square meters and is a two-storied brick-wood structure. The layout of the building is unsymmetrical and its exteriors are dry walls of glazed bricks. The terrace at the main entrance is supported by simplified Ionic columns and pilasters are arranged at the corner of the building. The multiple sloping roofs are covered with large arched tiles on which stands a dormant window. The building has overhanging eaves and the round tower on the roof top was damaged in the earthquake in 1976. The interior of the building is extravagantly decorated and the wooden stairs, floors, doors and windows remain intact until now. The whole building demonstrates the characteristics of British vernacular dwellings which feature simple architectural style and exquisite decoration in specific spot.

外景 Exterior view

外景 Exterior view

外景 Exterior view

原法国公议局

Former Municipal Administration of the French Concession

原法国公议局位于和平区承德道12号，全国重点文物保护单位，特殊保护等级历史风貌建筑，现为办公用房。法国公议局是原法租界董事会行使行政职能的执行机构，下分工程、捐务、会计三处。该建筑建于1931年，由比商义品公司门德森设计，占地面积约2 700 m^2，建筑面积约3 700 m^2。该建筑钢混结构，主体三层、两翼二层，设有地下室，外檐为水刷石断块墙面；其布局严谨对称，形体富于变化，墙面装饰丰富，线脚细腻，外观庄重大方，内装修富丽堂皇，带有典型的古典主义建筑特征。

Being the important heritage site under state protection and the special protection historic architecture in Tianjin, the site of the former Municipal Administration of the French Concession in Tianjin is located at No.12 Chengde Avenue, Heping District. Designed by L.Mendelssohn from a Belgian business—Credit Foncier D'Extreme Orient., the building was constructed in 1931. The building is used as an office building nowadays, covering an area of about 2,700 square meters, and about 3,700 square meters in floor area.

The administration was the executive body responsible for the Directorate of the French Concession in Tianjin, in charge of engineering, taxation and accountant.

Along with the basement and the outer-walls faced with granolithic blocks, the reinforced concrete structure is mainly three-storied but two-storied for its two wings. Rich in shape variation, architrave and wall decoration, the building is a symmetrical design. It looks tasteful outside and magnificent inside, presenting typically with the architectural classicism.

外檐吊灯
Hanging lamp under the outer-eaves

入口处内景
Inside view of the entrance

会议室 Meeting Room

原法国工部局
Former French Industry Bureau

原法国工部局位于和平区解放北路34~36号，天津市文物保护单位，特殊保护等级历史风貌建筑，现为办公用房。工部局原为法租界董事会下属工部局中的警察部，后单独改组为工部局，实为直接受法国驻津总领事馆领导的警察局。

该建筑建于1934年，占地面积约4 500 m^2，建筑面积约5 600 m^2，由比利时房产商义品公司设计建造，为四层混合结构楼房（设有半地下室）。建筑平面突出功能，立面造型采用古典三段式构图，屋顶采用法国19世纪末流行的孟莎式，兼具实用、装饰双重功能，墙面用清水红砖与混水装饰线搭配，大方明快。室内装修简洁，设施完善。

外景 Exterior view

外景 Exterior view

Situated at No.34~36 North Jiefang Road, Heping District, the former French Industry Bureau is the heritage site under city protection and the special protection historic architecture in Tianjin and it is now an office building. The bureau, used to be a police department of the Industry Bureau under the Board of Directors of the French Concession and later became an independent department called Industry Bureau, was actually the police bureau under the direct control of the French Consulate-general.

Established in 1934, the building covers an area of 4,500 square meters and has a floor area of 5,600 square meters. It was a four-storied mixed structure (with semi-basement) designed by the Credit Foncier d' Extreme Orient. The layout of the building is to maximize its function and the walls of the building adopt the classical three-partition structure. The roof of the building adopts Mansell style structure popular at the end of ninetieth century, which is both pragmatic and decorative. The walls of the building are constructed with dry wall made of red bricks and painted decorative ribs, giving it a dynamic and graceful look. The interior is well decorated and equipped with various facilities.

外檐吊灯
Hanging lamp under the outer-eaves

外檐窗
Windows below the outer-eaves

外景 Exterior view

原法国领事馆

Former French Consulate

原法国领事馆位于和平区承德道2号，天津市文物保护单位，特殊保护等级历史风貌建筑，现为办公用房。法国驻津领事馆是天津开埠后最早设立的领事馆之一，原馆址建于1861年，设在望海楼教堂以东的行宫花园（现河北区）。1869年丰大业任法国驻天津领事，在1870年“天津教案”事件中，丰大业持枪逞凶滋事，被天津民众殴毙，其后法国领事馆迁入现址。该建筑建于1923年，建筑面积约2 600 m^2，由比商义品公司设计。建筑形体简洁大方，立面设计丰富协调，外墙装饰西洋古典壁柱，纹样雕刻丰富，窗间墙及檐口部分均有精美花饰，具有典型的古典主义建筑特征。

Situated at No.2 Chengde Aveue, Heping District, Tianjin, the former French Consulate is the heritage site under city protection and the special protection historic architecture in Tianjin and it is now an office building. The French consulate is one of the first foreign consulates established in Tianjin since the city was opened as a commercial port. Constructed in 1861, the consulate was previously located at the Xinggong Garden (now Hebei District) to the east of the Wanghailou Church. In 1869, Henry Fontanier was appointed as the French consul to Tianjin and was beaten to death for shooting randomly at Chinese during Tianjin Massacre in 1870. Later the French Consulate was moved to the current place. This building, designed by the Credit Foncier D'Extreme Orient and constructed in 1923, has a floor area of 2,600 square meters. It has a simple look and coordinated facade design. The building is a typical classical building featuring exterior walls decorated with classic pilasters with rich carvings and exquisitely decorated eaves and walls between the windows.

外景 Exterior view

原意大利领事馆
Former Italian Consulate

原意大利领事馆位于河北区建国道52号，天津市文物保护单位，重点保护等级历史风貌建筑，现为办公用房。该建筑建于1909年，为意大利政府驻津领事馆。1945年后，作为二战的战败国，意大利政府将意租界交回中国政府，领事馆亦撤销。该建筑建筑面积约1 200 m^2，砖木结构二层楼房，清水砖墙，瓦屋面四坡顶，屋檐出挑较大，舒展平缓。主入口门套、窗套及墙面转角等部位，采用意大利古典建筑的装饰手法，简洁明快。室内装饰豪华，使用功能合理，建筑整体设计舒展大方。

Located at No.52 Jianguo Avenue, Hebei District, Tianjin, the former Italian Consulate is the heritage site under city protection and the important protection historic architecture in Tianjin and it serves as an office building now. The building, constructed in 1909, served as the Italian Consulate to Tianjin. After 1945, the Italian government, defeated in the Second World War, returned the Italian Concession to Chinese government and the Italian Consulate, as a result, ceased to exist. The building, having a floor area of about 1,200 square meters, is a two-storied brick-wood structure featuring fair-faced walls, hip roof covered with tiles and long overhanging eaves. The door profile, windows profile and corners of the main entrance are neatly decorated, following the Italian classical architectural style. The rooms of the building are extravagantly decorated with function properly so the building is well-stretched and graceful.

内景 Inside view

正立面外景 Facade view

背立面外景 Back view

原俄国领事馆

Former Russian Consulate

原俄国领事馆位于河东区十一经路88号，天津市文物保护单位，重点保护等级历史风貌建筑，现为办公用房。1902—1903年，沙俄政府在俄租界海河渡口附近修建了该领事馆，1917年俄国十月革命后，改为苏联驻津总领事馆。1924年，苏联政府放弃租界权力，领事馆另作他用。1942年成为日本海关办事机构。该建筑平面呈凹字形，建筑面积约1 800 m^2，正立面朝海河，侧立面临十一经路大光明桥。砖木结构二层楼房，混水墙面，瓦屋面坡顶；主、侧入口均为拱券门，上有挑梁支撑的阳台，窗户设三角形、一字形石窗楣；首层窗台及窗套、角柱等均为石材砌筑，墙面粘贴黄色瓷砖。

Standing at No.88 Shiyijing Road, Hedong District, Tianjin, the former Russian Consulate is the heritage site under city protection and the important protection historic architecture in Tianjin and it is now an office building. From 1902 to 1903, the Russian government built this consulate at the ferry of Haihe River in the Russian Concession. After the October Revolution in 1917, the consulate became the Soviet Union's consulate-general to Tianjin. In 1924, the Soviet Union gave up its concession right and the consulate was used for other purposes. In 1942, the building became an office building of Japanese customs. Having a floor area of 1,800 square meters, the building is concave-shaped and faces the Haihe River. One side of the building faces the Daguangming Bridge on the Haihe River. The two-storied brick-wood structure has plastered brick walls and sloping roof covered with tiles. The main and side entrances of the building are arched and topped with balcony supported by the overhanging beams. The windows are equipped with triangular and horizontal stone window lintels. The window sill, exterior window trim and corner post are all made with stone. The walls are decorated with yellow ceramic tiles.

楼梯 Stairs

主入口
Main entrancev

原汇丰银行

Former Hongkong and Shanghai Bank Corporation

汇丰银行创办于1864年，总行设在香港。天津分行于1881年开业，为天津第一家外商银行，是天津对外贸易的主要结算银行，获有中国关税、盐税的托管权，享有纸币发行权，决定着天津的外汇市场，1954年撤离。该建筑位于和平区解放北路82号，天津市文物保护单位，特殊保护等级历史风貌建筑，现为中国银行。其建于1925年，占地面积约2 900 m^2，建筑面积约4 300 m^2，由英商爱迪克生和达拉斯（同和）工程司设计，为钢混结构三层楼房。建筑正面及侧面矗立十二根巨大的爱奥尼克石柱，体现出古罗马柱式的高大雄伟，属典型的古典主义风格。

Hongkong and Shanghai Bank Corporation (HSBC) was founded in 1864 with its headquarters in Hong Kong. HSBC Tianjin Branch opened in 1881, being the first foreign capital bank in the city. It served as the main international settlement & trustee bank, dealing with the foreign trade, custom duty & salt tax, and banknote issue in the city.

Before it ended its business in 1954, the bank was located at No.82 North Jiefang Road, Heping District. Designed by the English designing body, Atkinson & Dallas Architects and Civil Engineers Ltd., the building constructed in 1925 has been listed as the heritage site under city protection and the special protection historic architecture in Tianjin. Now, the building is used by Bank of China, covering an area of about 2,900 square meters, and about 4,300 square meters in floor area.

With 12 massive Ionic columns erecting along its facade and sides in the ancient Roman orders, the three-storied reinforced concrete structure looks grand and majestic. It is featured to be in a classical style.

外景 Exterior view

中國銀行

营业厅内景
Inside Business Hall

appy New Year
新年快乐
银行卡开销户
57
58
59
60

外景 Exterior view

原麦加利银行

Former Chartered Bank of India,Australia and China

麦加利银行（亦称“渣打银行”），创办于1853年，总行设在伦敦，是英国皇家特许的殖民地银行。天津分行于1895年开业，主要业务为定活期存款、汇兑信用证，1954年关闭。该建筑位于和平区解放北路149~153号，天津市文物保护单位，特殊保护等级历史风貌建筑，现为办公用房。建筑建于1926年，占地面积约2 300 m^2，建筑面积约5 600 m^2，由英商赫明与帕尔克因（景明）工程公司设计，二层钢混结构楼房（设有地下室）。建筑主入口由六根爱奥尼克式巨柱形成开敞柱廊，气势宏伟庄严，建筑整体感很强，具有典型的古典主义风格。

Also known as the Standard Chartered Bank, the Chartered Bank of India, Australia and China was founded via the approval of the English Royalty in 1853 with its headquarters located in London. It could be identified by its name as one of the chartered banks specially operating in the English colonies. It opened its Tianjin Branch in 1895, with the business scope covering the current deposit and exchanging LC (Letter of Credit), etc. The Branch ends its business in 1954. The building formerly serving for the Branch is located at No.149~153 North Jiefang Road, Heping District. It has been regarded as the heritage site under city protection and the special protection historic architecture in Tianjin. Now, the building is used as an office building, covering an area of about 2,300 square meters, and about 5,600 square meters in floor area.

The three-storied building was designed by the Hemmings & Parkin Ltd., an English engineering company. The open colonnade with 6 massive Ionic columns is added to the Main Entrance of this reinforced concrete structure, looking more majestic and spectacular as a whole. It is a classical architecture in style.

外景 Exterior view

外景 Exterior view

原中法工商银行

Former French Chinese Bank

原中法工商银行于1923年由中法实业银行改组而成，为中法合资银行，在上海、天津、北京等地设有分行。天津分行于1925年开业，1948 年停业。该建筑位于和平区解放北路74~78 号，天津市文物保护单位，特殊保护等级历史风貌建筑，现为办公用房。其始建于1919年，1932－1933年、1936年增建，四层混和结构楼房（设有地下室），局部五层。占地面积约1 600 m^2，建筑面积约5 000 m^2。建筑主入口设于街角，两侧通廊由沿弧线对称布置的十根科林斯巨柱构成，气势宏伟，造型典雅别致，具有典型的古典主义风格。

The former French-Chinese Bank of Commerce and Industry was reorganized from the Banque Industrielle de Chine in 1923. It was a joint-venture bank and had run its branches in Shanghai, Beijing and Tianjin , etc.. The Tianjin Branch opened in 1925 and ended its business in 1948.

The building formerly serving as the Bank's site sits at 74~78 North Jiefang Road, Heping District, as one of the heritage site under city protection and the special protection historic architecture in Tianjin. This building was initially built in 1919 and expanded in 1932-1933 and 1936 respectively. Now, the building is used as an office building, covering an area of about 1,600 square meters, and about 5,000 square meters in floor area. The composite structure is mainly four-storied but five-storied partially (with basement). The main entrance is designed at the corner with ten massive Corinthian columns standing symmetrically along its sides, forming the open colonnade. The whole building looks significant and elegant, presenting with the classical atmosphere.

壁柱柱式 Pilaster

机动车
禁止通行

外景 Exterior view

侧立面 Side elevation

原东方汇理银行
Former L'indo Bank of China

原东方汇理银行位于和平区解放北路77~79号，天津市文物保护单位，重点保护等级历史风貌建筑，现为办公用房。东方汇理银行创办于1875年，总行设于法国巴黎。20世纪初先后在我国上海、天津、北京、汉口、广州等地建立分行。天津分行1907年开业，主要经营进出口押汇及买卖外汇。1913年曾代表法国参与五国银行团，与北洋政府签订了“善后大借款”。1957年停业。该建筑1912年建成，占地面积约1 200 m^2，建筑面积约3 500 m^2，由比商义品公司设计。砖木结构三层楼房，建筑首层为水泥仿石块墙面，二、三层为清水红砖墙与混水墙面搭配，墙面装饰有抹灰纹样；建筑造型稳重，细部丰富，色彩明快大方，具有西洋古典主义建筑特征。

The former L'indo Bank of China was situated at No.77~79 North Jiefang Road, Heping District. It is now the heritage site under city protection and the important protection historic architecture in Tianjin and used as an office building. The L'indo Bank of China was established in Paris in 1875. In the early twentieth century, branches of the bank were set up in Shanghai, Tianjin, Beijing, Hankou, Guangzhou, etc. The Tianjin branch opened in 1907 and specialized in inward documentary bills, outward documentary bills and foreign exchange trading. In 1913, the bank signed the Reorganization Loan Agreement together as the French member of the Consortia of Five Banks. The bank was closed down in 1957. The office building of the L'indo Bank of China was designed by Credit Foncier d'Extreme Orient and built in 1912, covering an area of about 1,200 square meters and creating a floor area of about 3,500 square meters. The walls of the first floor were covered with stone-like concrete and those of the second and third floors were red brick and furred walls. It belongs to the Western classical architecture style.

外景 Exterior view

西洋美术馆

原金城银行

Former Kinchen Bank

原金城银行大楼位于和平区解放北路108号，天津市文物保护单位，重点保护等级历史风貌建筑，现为办公用房。金城银行开业于1917年，由中国近代银行家周作民创办，发起人为倪嗣冲、任凤苞、胡笔江等，行名取“金城汤池永久坚固之意”，总行设于天津，1936年迁往上海。金城银行是近代中国著名的民族资本商业银行，也是北四行（金城、盐业、大陆、中南）的核心和支柱。1952年加入金融业全行业公私合营后宣告结束。

金城银行大楼建于1937年，占地面积约4 500m^2，建筑面积约3 200m^2，由中国第一代著名建筑师——华信工程司沈理源先生设计。建筑为二层砖木结构，带地下室，外墙装饰面砖；布局规整对称，造型为古典复兴与民居建筑的混合，立面装饰丰富。

Situated at No.108 North Jiefang Road, Heping District, the former Kinchen Bank is now the heritage site under city protection and the important protection historic architecture and is currently used as an office building. The former Kinchen Bank was established in Tianjin in 1917 by Zhou Zuomin, Ni Sichong, Ren Fengbao and Hu Bijiang. In 1936, the bank was relocated to Shanghai. Kinchen Bank was the core of the "four northern banks" in modern China (the other three were Salt Industry Bank, Continuental Bank and China & South Sea Bank). In 1952, it was grouped into the "Joint Office of Joint Public-Private Banks" with other eight Chinese banks. The former Kinchen Bank building was built by Huaxin Engineering Company in 1937 following the design of Shen Liyuan, China's first generation designer and it covers an area of 4,500 square meters and its floor area is 3,200 square meters. This two-storied brick-wood building with a basement was laid out in perfect symmetry and its exterior walls were covered with decorative tiles. As it combined the classical revival style and vernacular dwelling, its facads were beautifully decorated.

围墙 Enclosure

外景 Exterior view

外景 Exterior view

原朝鲜银行

Former Korean Bank

原朝鲜银行位于和平区解放北路97~101号，天津市文物保护单位，特殊保护等级历史风貌建筑，现为办公、居住混合用房。朝鲜银行由日本投资，1911年在朝鲜京城建立总行，天津分行于1918年开业。抗日战争胜利后，由中国政府按敌伪产业予以接收。该建筑建于1918年，占地面积约1 100 m^2，建筑面积约3 500 m^2，混合结构三层楼房。虽为仿希腊古典复兴建筑风格，但外檐墙面、柱式均采用清水红砖，体现了地方材料和鲜明的个性，色彩明快温馨；主入口设于转角处，建筑体量处理简洁明快，细部处理精致协调。

The former Korean Bank, situated at No.97~101 North Jiefang Road, Heping District, is now the heritage site under city protection and the special protection historic architecture in Tianjin and is used as an office and residential building. It was a Japanese-funded bank established in the capital of Korea in 1911. The Tianjin branch opened in 1918. After the victory of the Anti-Japanese War, the Chinese government confiscated the bank as Japanese property. This building was built in 1918, covering an area of some 1,100 square meters and producing the floor area of about 3,500 square meters. It is a three-storied building of the classical Revival style. The red brick exterior walls and pillars exhibit unique local charming. It is a perfect combination of a simple framework and exquisite details.

外檐局部

Partial outer-eaves

主入口门 Main Entrance

原横滨正金银行

Former Yokohama Specie Bank Limited

横滨正金银行创办于1880年，总部设在日本横滨。天津分行成立于1899年，以经营外汇及存贷款为主要业务，曾在中国发行钞票。通过贷款、透支，支持日商大量向中国华北输出商品，获得廉价原料，牟取暴利。抗战胜利后，由中国银行接收。

该建筑位于和平区解放北路80号，天津市文物保护单位，特殊保护等级历史风貌建筑，现为中国银行。其建于1926年，占地面积约2 700 m^2，建筑面积约5 000 m^2，由英商爱迪克生和达拉斯（同和）工程司设计，为三层混合结构楼房；建筑外檐为石材墙面，造型稳重华丽，其正立面的八根科林斯巨柱构成的开敞柱廊强调了对称构图，具有典型的古典主义风格。

The bank was established in 1880 with its headquarters in Yokohama, Japan. Its Tianjin Branch was founded in 1899. Its business scope was mainly related with foreign exchange, deposit and loan. And the bank also issued the banknotes in China. By means of loan and overdraft, the bank supported the Japanese merchants for exporting their goods to North China and obtaining the cheaper raw materials from China in order to seek excessive profits. After the Anti-Japanese War, the Bank was taken over by Bank of China.

Located at No.80 North Jiefang Road and built in 1926, the building once occupied by the Japanese Bank was designed by the English designing body, Atkinson & Dallas Architects and Civil Engineers Ltd. It is opened as the heritage site under city protection and the special protection historic architecture in Tianjin. Now, the building is used by Bank of China, covering an area of about 2,700 square meters, and about 5,000 square meters in floor area.

The outer-eaves of this three-storied composite structure are decorated with stone facings, looking steady and smart. A grand colonnade presents with 8 massive Corinthian columns standing symmetrically along the facade of the building. It could be considered as a typical Western architecture in the classical form.

贵宾室
Room for the honored guests

外景 Exterior view

中國銀行

塔楼
Roof tower (helmet-shaped roof)

原华俄道胜银行

Former Russo-Chinese Bank

华俄道胜银行由法国和俄国银行业发起成立，总行设在俄罗斯圣彼得堡。天津分行于1896年开业，以发行的卢布为主要交易筹码，进行投机买卖，代办中国各种税款，1926年停业。该建筑位于和平区解放北路121号，天津市文物保护单位，特殊保护等级历史风貌建筑，现为中国人民银行。其建于1900年，占地面积约700 m^2，建筑面积约2 900 m^2。二层砖木结构楼房。建筑外檐墙面饰以黄色面砖，券形窗口、饰有人字形山花的平窗、弧形转角及盔顶构成一座具有浓郁的俄罗斯风格的古典主义建筑，室内装修讲究，大量精美木饰保存完好。

The bank was originally founded by means of the joint Franco-Russian capital with its headquarters in St. Petersburg, Russia. It opened its Tianjin Branch in 1896, mainly dealing with the Chinese tax affairs and issuing Rubles to aid its speculative transactions in China. It was closed in 1926.

Originally built in 1900, the bank is located at No.121 North Jiefang Road, Heping District. It has been regarded as the heritage site under city protection and the special protection historic architecture in Tianjin. Now, the building is used by the People's Bank of China, covering an area of about 700 square meters, and about 2,900 square meters in floor area.

This two-storied brick-wood structure was designed classically in a typical Russian style, with yellow-faced walls, arched windows accompanied with the pedimental windows and curving corners along with huge helmet-shaped roof. The interior decorations have been regarded to be the most elegant and a lot of wooden structure have been preserved quite well till now.

塔楼内木结构

Wooden structures inside the roof tower

外景 Exterior view

主入口外景 Main entrance

原盐业银行

Former Salt Industry Bank

盐业银行创办于1915年，总行设在北京，是中国著名的商业银行，同年天津分行开业。初系“盐务专业银行”，后改“招商股”，成为普通商业银行，与金城、大陆、中南三家银行并称为“北四行”。该建筑位于和平区赤峰道12号，全国重点文物保护单位，特殊保护等级历史风貌建筑，建于1926年，现为中国工商银行，占地面积约2 100 m^2，建筑面积约6 200 m^2。由华信工程司建筑师沈理源设计，四层砖混平顶楼房（设有地下室和中二层）。建筑主入口为通高的神庙式门厅，正立面用六根混合式巨柱支撑形成开敞长廊；墙面为水刷石饰面，饰以精美雕刻。建筑采用三段式构图，具有典型的古典主义特征，气势宏伟，装饰丰富，线脚细腻，富丽堂皇。

The same year when initially established, the Salt Industry Bank opened its branch in Tianjin in 1915. It was well-known as a commercial bank with its headquarters located in Beijing then. It was serving specially for salt affairs at the beginning and turned to an ordinary commercial bank later, being one of the four most famous banks in North China along with the Kinchen Bank, Continental Bank and China & South Sea Bank Ltd.

The site of the bank sits at No.12 Chifeng Avenue, Heping District, which has been listed as the important heritage site under state protection and the special protection historic architecture in Tianjin. Now, the building is used by Industrial and Commercial Bank of China, covering an area of about 2,100 square meters, and about 6,200 square meters in floor area.

As one of the splendid works of Mr. Shen Liyuan, a Chinese architect, the building was originally built in 1926. The four-storied brick-concrete architecture is composed classically of three sections with its basement and intermediate-layer on the second floor as well. It looks more magnificent for its extractive designs: main entrance formed in highly fane-style, facade colonnade structured by six massive columns, walls faced with granite-plaster, and the whole building decorated with delicate architrave, rich carvings and elegant architraves.

外景 Exterior view

原东莱银行
Former Tunglai Bank

原东莱银行位于和平区和平路287号，天津市文物保护单位，重点保护等级历史风貌建筑，现为办公用房。东莱银行为中资银行，成立于1918年，1919年设立天津分行，1953年结业。建于1930年，占地面积约3 300 m²，建筑面积约7 500 m²，由贝伦特工程司设计，大楼建成后东莱银行从宫北大街旧址迁入新楼。该建筑为混合结构三层楼房，局部四层，混水墙面。主入口两侧为贯通两层的科林斯柱廊，檐部为山花，具有典型的仿希腊古典复兴建筑特征。入口处的阁楼层上设高耸的重檐圆形塔楼，使建筑主入口突出，同时建筑形式也增加了折中主义的成分。室内装饰考究，营业大厅内为彩色水磨石地面、大理石护墙板，充分显示了银行的实力。

Former Tunglai Bank, a Chinese-funded bank established in 1918, had its Tianjin branch set up at No.287 Heping Road, Heping District in 1919. Its former site is now the heritage site under city protection and the important protection historic architecture in Tianjin and is used as an office building. It was closed down in 1953. The office building of former Tung Lai Bank was designed and built by Behrendt Engineering Company in 1930. It covers an area of about 3,300 square meters and has a floor area of about 7,500 square meters. This three-storied mixed structure with part of the building being four-storied has plastered brick walls, Corinthian colonnades at the main entrance and pediment at the top of the front, which belongs to the revival of classical Greece style. Meanwhile, elements of eclecticism were also added as a multiple-eave round tower was built on the attic over the main entrance to give prominence to it. Besides, the colored terrazzo floor and marble wall panel demonstrated the financial power of the bank.

外景 Exterior view

原新华信托储蓄银行
Former Sinhua Trust Savings Bank

原新华信托储蓄银行位于和平区解放北路10号，天津市文物保护单位，重点保护等级历史风貌建筑，现为办公用房。新华信托储蓄银行由中资中国银行、交通银行于1919年联合创办，原名“新华储蓄银行”，1931年改组后更名为“新华信托储蓄银行”。该行以“提倡社会储蓄，培养人民俭德”为宗旨，天津分行主要业务为存放款及储蓄，兼营经收信托款项、买卖有价证券、房地产、保险等业务，并发行流通储蓄券，后又推出整借零还小额贷款，首创人寿储金、生活储金、教育储金。据原中国人民银行参事室主任、中国银行界元老沈日新老人回忆，新华信托储蓄银行当时还有一项重要的业务，即所有的中资银行每天下午4点均要到该行来进行汇总结账，沟通情况，可以说是天津中资银行的大本营。1952年该银行结业。该建筑建于1934年，占地面积约1 100 m²，建筑面积约9 200 m²，由华信工程司建筑师沈理源设计，正门设于解放北路与滨江道转角处，营业大厅贯通一、二层，主体六层，局部八层，钢筋混凝土框架结构，外檐石材饰面，建筑造型庄重挺拔，强调竖向构图，整体感很强，是20世纪诞生的现代建筑的典型代表。

The former Sinhua Trust Saving Bank, situated at No.10 North Jiefang Road, Heping District, is now the heritage site under city protection and the important protection historic architecture in Tianjin and used as an office building now. The Sin Hua Trust Savings Bank, previously Sin Hua Savings Bank, was established by Chinese-funded Bank of China and Bank of Communications in 1919 and renamed as the Sin Hua Trust Savings Bank after its reorganization in 1931. The bank advocated a savers' society. Its Tianjin branch first engaged in mainly deposit, loan, savings, trust payment, securities dealing, real estate and insurance. Later it issued savings certificates, promoted a service of petty loan, and initiated life insurance savings, life savings and education savings.

Shen Rixin, one of the earliest financial experts in China, head of the advisory office of the People's Bank of China recalled that the Sin Hua Trust Savings Bank was the base camp of all the Chinese-funded banks in Tianjin because officers from all the banks got together to settle account and exchange information everyday at 4 o'clock. In 1952, the Sin Hua Trust Savings Bank was closed down.

The building was designed by Shen Liyuan and built by Huaxin Engineering Company in 1934. It covers about 1,100 square meters and has a floor area of about 9,200 square meters. The main entrance is at the corner of North Jiefang Road and Binjiang Avenue. The business hall is two-storied high and the main body of the reinforced concrete building is six-storied while part of it is eight-storied. The stone-decorated facade had highlighted the vertical format and made the building a classic representative of modern architectures in the twentieth Century.

主入口外景
Exterior view of the main entrance

利顺德大饭店
Astor House Hotel

利顺德大饭店位于和平区解放北路199号，全国重点文物保护单位，特殊保护等级历史风貌建筑，创建于1863年，是中国近代首家外商开办的大饭店。孙中山先生、美国前总统胡佛等曾在此下榻。该饭店初为平房，1884年扩建为英国古典式三层楼房，是当时英租界最大最高的建筑。1929年增建四层楼房，经多次改造，现两座建筑保存完好，占地面积约3 900 m^2，建筑面积约10 500 m^2；位于街角的三层楼房，建筑造型稳重大方，舒展挺拔，转角处方形角楼强化了竖向构图，外墙装饰丰富且手法简洁，运用了许多古典建筑符号。

Regarded as the important heritage site under state protection and the special protection historic architecture in Tianjin, the Astor House Hotel is located at No.199 North Jiefang Road, Heping District, covering an area of about 3,900 square meters, and about 10,500 square meters in floor area. Many great figures have once stayed at the hotel, such as Mr. Sun Yat-sen and Hoover, deceased former president of U.S.

Being the first large-scale hotel operated by the foreigners in the contemporary China, the hotel was founded in 1863 in bungalow-style and expanded to be three-storied hotel in English classical-style in 1884 which was the tallest building in the British concession at that time. Once more in 1929, the hotel was reconstructed to be four-storied. Both of the buildings have been preserved very well.

The three-storied building at the street corner was massive and decent. Its quadrate turret at the turning point was aimed at enhancing visually the vertical sense of the structure. The walls were finished richly but simple. A lot of classical architectural signs were adapted to the designing of the building.

西餐厅 Western dining-hall

夜景 Night view

老楼梯 Old-fashioned stair

老电梯 Old-fashioned elevator

外景 Exterior view

原泰莱饭店
Former Talati House Hotel

原泰莱饭店位于和平区解放北路158号，重点保护等级历史风貌建筑，现为天津第一饭店。饭店创办人泰莱悌为印度流浪汉，原籍孟买，20世纪初来津，初开设小卖部，后开设永昌泰洋行，富裕后加入英国籍转向房地产业。1929年泰莱悌与英国人莱德劳合股筹建泰莱饭店，后泰莱悌设法赶走合伙人，独占了该饭店。1936年，泰莱悌取得了饭店北侧的土地，并增建了六层楼房，与既有建筑连成一体，成为当时规模较大的综合性饭店，占地面积约1 800 m^2，建筑面积约7 600 m^2。该建筑由比商义品公司设计，钢筋混凝土框架结构，外檐立面设计简洁，大面积粘贴黄褐色麻面面砖，相间布置水刷石方壁柱，局部装饰简约古典纹样；建筑整体感强，造型典雅，色彩和谐，具有典型的现代建筑特征。

The former Talati House Hotel, now Tianjin First Hotel was situated at No.158 North Jiefang Road, Heping District and it is now an important protection historic architecture in Tianjin. S.B.Talatl, the founder of the hotel, used to be an Indian tramp in Bombay. In the early 1900s, he came to China and first started running a small shop and then Talati Estates Limited. After he earned his first barrel of gold, Talati managed to become a British citizen and set his foot in real estate. In 1929, Talati and Laidlaw, a British joined hands to build the Talati House Hotel. But later Talati drove his partner away and made the hotel his own. In 1936, Talati built a six-storied building to the north of the hotel and joined the two buildings to a larger hotel which covers an area of about 1,800 square meters and has a floor area of about 7,600 square meters. This reinforced concrete frame building was designed by the Credit Foncier d'Extreme Orient. With most of its facade covered with tawny pitting surface front bricks alternating with square granitic plasters, and plain classic patterns as decoration, the Talati House Hotel looks elegant and its harmonious colors and sense of unity emphasize the characteristics of modern architecture.

原惠中饭店

Former Huizhong Hotel

原惠中饭店位于和平区滨江道141~153号、华中路2号、和平路292号，天津市文物保护单位,重点保护等级历史风貌建筑，现为商业用房。该建筑建于1930年，1931年开业，由上海华中营造公司驻津工程部设计，占地面积约为2 100 m^2，建筑面积约为11 000 m^2，是当时天津最著名的饭店之一。为适应当时租界社会不同层次的娱乐与休闲需求，饭店设有中西餐部、舞厅、露天影院、露天球场等，出入者多为军阀政客、工商业人士、社会白领等。著名作家曹禺曾以其为社会生活背景，创作出话剧《日出》。该建筑为混合结构建筑，主体五层，局部六层，中部更在六层之上设高耸的三层塔楼，是典型的折中主义建筑形式。

外景 Exterior view

Located at 141~153 Binjiang Avenue, No.2 Huazhong Road and No.292 Heping Road of Heping District, the former Huizhong Hotel is now the heritage site under city protection and the important protection historic architecture in Tianjin and is used for business. Designed by the Tianjin Branch of Shanghai Huazhong Construction Company, Huizhong Hotel was built in 1930 and came into use in 1931. Covering an area of about 2,100 square meters and a floor area of about 11,000 square meters, it was then one of the most well-known restaurants in Tianjin. To meet different requirements of the concessions in Tianjin, dance hall, open cinema, Chinese cuisine and Western cuisine were available to the guests, most of whom were warlords, politicians, businessmen and elites. With the story happened in this hotel as the original material, Cao Yu, the great playwright, wrote out *Sunrise*. The former Huizhong Hotel was a five-storied building, part of which was six-storied, with a three-storied high tower on the top, belonging to the eclectic architecture.

外景 Exterior view

原国民饭店

Former National Grand Hotel

国民饭店位于和平区赤峰道58号，天津市文物保护单位，重点保护等级历史风貌建筑，为中国商人租用陆安公司土地投资建造的，是当时天津豪华饭店之一，现为商业用房。1926年中国共产党在此召开了中华全国铁路总工会第三次代表大会；1934年，爱国将领吉鸿昌在此从事抗日活动时被国民党特务刺伤并逮捕；抗日战争期间，中共天津市委秘密机关和联络站“知识书店”也设于此。该建筑建于1923年，占地面积约为3 100 m^2，建筑面积约为6 400 m^2，由乐利工程司设计，原设计四层，实际建造为三层，钢筋混凝土内框架结构，平屋顶，檐部出挑，建筑南立面采用对称构图，纵横三段式；院落宽敞，内设半球形盔顶凉亭两座，正门为塔什干柱式支撑的门楼，庄重大方。

The former National Grand Hotel was situated at No.58 Chifeng Avenue in Heping District. It is the heritage site under city protection and the important protection historic architecture in Tianjin and is now used for business. It used to be one of the most luxurious hotels in Tianjin and was built on the land rented from Lu'an Company by a Chinese merchant. In 1926, the Chinese Communist Party held the third Plenary Session of All-China Federation of Railway Workers Union here and in 1934 Ji Hongchang, the patriotic general, was stabbed and arrested by the agents of KMT in this hotel. During the War of Resistance against Japan, the secret office of Tianjin municipal Party committee and the liaison location—Knowledge Bookstore were both located here. This three-storied hotel with a floor area of about 6,400 square meters was built in 1923, taking up an area of about 3,100 square meters. However, it was originally designed as four-storied by Leli Engineering Company. It is a reinforced concrete inner frame structure construction with a flat roof, overhanging eaves and a gateway supported by Tashkent pillars.Two semi-arch arbors are found inside the yard. The building is symmetrical, elegant and spacious.

主入口 Main Entrance

外景 Exterior view

劝业场
Quanyechang Mall

劝业场建于1928年，是当时华北地区规模最大的百货商场，“天津劝业场”匾额为著名书法家华世奎所书。场内设有天华景戏院、天宫影院、天乐评戏院等8个娱乐场所，合称“八大天”，集购物、娱乐、休闲于一体，是中华著名商业老字号，并一度成为天津的象征。该建筑位于和平区滨江道152~166号，全国重点文物保护单位，特殊保护等级历史风貌建筑，由法籍工程师穆乐设计、法商永和营造公司建造，占地面积约3 000 m^2，建筑面积约16 500 m^2。建筑为框架结构五层楼房（局部八层），石材饰面，窗户形式多样，建筑形式带有折中主义色彩。

丰富的外檐装饰
Luxuriant designs of the outer-eaves

天津勸業場
KFC

Being the largest scale department store in North China founded in 1928, the Quanyechang Mall was honored with a tablet inscribed by Mr. Hua Shikui, one of the most famous calligraphers in China. Eight grand recreation groups all named with "Tian" got together in the store, including Tian-huajing Theatre, Tian-fu Cinema, and Tain-le Stage for Ping Opera, etc. The mall could serve the people for their shopping, enjoyment and amusement all within its body. Well-known as one of the outstanding enterprises with long history in China and one of the symbols for the city, it has been classified as the important heritage site under state protection and the special protection historic architecture in Tianjin, covering an area of about 3,000 square meters, and about 16,500 square meters in floor area.

Located at No.152~166 Binjiang Avenue of Heping District, the building was designed by Mr. P. Muller, the architect from a French engineering company-Hunke & Muller. The building is mainly five-storied and eight-storied partially and has got its walls finished with stone facing. And it has its windows in various forms. The whole architecture tastes to be somewhat eclectic considering its designs.

夜景 Night view

丰富的外檐装饰
Luxuriant designs of the outer-eaves

塔楼 Towered roof

外景 Exterior view

渤海大楼
Bohai Building

渤海大楼位于和平区和平路275~281号，天津市文物保护单位，特殊保护等级历史风貌建筑，建于1936年，由法商永和营造公司设计，是当时天津最高、最新式的商业、公寓混合大楼，也是当时天津市中心的标志性建筑，现为商业用房。该建筑为钢混框架结构八层楼房（局部十层），高47.47 m，占地面积约500 m^2，建筑面积约4 500 m^2；外墙面粘贴褐色饰面砖，色彩稳重大方；建筑立面强调竖向构图，体量庄重挺拔，属典型的现代主义风格。

Being the heritage site under city protection and the special protection historic architecture in Tianjin, Bohai Building sits at No.275~281 Heping Road, Heping District. Now, the building is used as commercial building, covering an area of about 500 square meters, and about 4,500 square meters in floor area.

Bohai Building was designed by the French engineering company—Hunke & Muller and built in 1936. It served both for commerce and resident, regarded as the highest and the modernist building in the city and as symbolic construction of the downtown.

This reinforced concrete structure is mainly eight-storied and partially ten-storied. Its walls were finished with brown tile facing, looking more massive and elegant. Vertical format was adopted for its designing, making the building taste highly-erective visually. It is regarded to be in modern style typically.

塔楼 Roof tower

广东会馆
Guangdong Guild Hall

广东会馆位于南开区南门里街31号，全国重点文物保护单位，特殊保护等级历史风貌建筑，现为戏剧博物馆。该会馆建于1907年，由天津海关道唐绍仪等倡议集资兴建，是旅津广东人议事集会的场所。该建筑群是天津现存规模最大、装饰最精美的会馆。1912 年孙中山曾在这里发表演说；1919年邓颖超曾领导觉悟社成员在这里进行募捐义演；1925年中共领导的天津总工会在这里成立；孙菊仙、杨小楼、梅兰芳、荀慧生等京剧大师都曾在此馆演出。整个建筑群采用中国传统的合院建筑形式，具有广东潮州四合院的建筑特征；砖木结构，重要的房间和门窗均有精美的砖雕、木雕；会馆内的戏楼采用穹隆状密集旋转斗拱藻井，装饰华美。

外景 Exterior view

The Guangdong Guild Hall is located at No.31 Inner Nanmen Street, Nankai District, classified as the important heritage site under state protection and the special protection historic architecture in Tianjin, and it is used as theater museum right now. The hall was constructed in 1907, sponsored by Tang Shaoyi, the governor of Tianjin Customs, and his fellows. It served the people from Guangdong Province for their gatherings. It is regarded as the biggest and best-decorated guild-building complex among this type of the constructions preserved in Tianjin. It was the place where Dr. Sun Yat-sen gave his speech in 1912, Madam Deng Yingchao with the members of her Consciousness Organization came to send round the hat in 1919 and the Tianjin Federation of Trade Unions under the leadership of the Chinese Communist Party was founded. Moreover, many masters of the Peking Opera gave their performances here, such as Sun Juxian, Yang Xiaolou, Mei Lanfang and Xun Huisheng, etc. The complex is a design of a Chinese traditional enclosing layout, further with the characters of the courtyard houses in Chaozhou Area of Guangdong Province. It is brick-wood structured. Elegant carvings made of brick and wood would be seen anywhere from the main rooms and their doors/windows. Brackets and coffers in special shapes were arranged densely against the arched roof, in order to enhance the effects not only of the decoration but also of the acoustics.

戏楼内景/Interior view of the hall

戏台藻井
Coffered ceiling above the stage

府庙棂星门
Lingxing Gate of the Prefecture Temple

文　庙
Confucian Temple

文庙，也称“孔庙”，为祭祀孔子的场所。天津文庙位于南开区东门里大街1号，天津市文物保护单位，特殊保护等级历史风貌建筑。该建筑群由府庙、县庙、明伦堂组成，按照中国传统的古建筑营造体制建造。文庙始建于明正统元年（1436年），当时称“卫学”，清雍正年间，天津卫逐渐升为府，该庙则归天津府管理，称“府庙”。天津府的首县即天津县，因府县官员不可同祭孔子，雍正十二年（1734年）在府庙西侧另建文庙，由天津县管理，称“县庙”。由此形成了天津文庙府县并存的格局。两庙均由万仞宫墙、泮池、棂星门、大成门、大成殿、崇圣祠和东西两侧配殿等组成。县庙为青砖青瓦，体量较小。府庙体量较大，中轴线建筑为黄琉璃瓦顶。文庙是明清两代至民国初年期间天津于春秋两季举行祭孔大典的场所，现为“文庙博物馆”。

Confucian Temple (also called Wen Temple) is a place to offer sacrifices to Confucius. Standing at No.1 Inner DongMen Street, Nankai District, Tianjin, the temple is the heritage site under city protection and the special protection historic architecture in Tianjin. The temple, constructed by following the style of traditional Chinese architectural complex, consists of Prefecture Temple, County Temple and Minglun Hall. Established in 1436 (the first year of Zhengtong's Reign, Ming Dynasty), the Confucian Temple was known as a garrison school (Wei Xue) at that time. During the reign of Yongzheng Emperor of Qing Dynasty, Tianjin was promoted from a garrison to a prefecture and the temple was put under the control of Tianjin prefecture. Since then it started to be called the Prefecture Temple (Fu Miao).

In ancient China, officials of different levels couldn't offer sacrifice to Confucius in a same temple and the first county under the Tianjin prefecture's control is Tianjin County. Therefore, in 1734 (the twelfth year of Yongzheng's Reign, Qing Dynasty), the Confucian Temple (Wen Miao) was established to the west of the Prefecture Temple (Fu Miao) and was called County Temple (Xian Temple) under the control of Tianjin County. This is why two Confucian Temples at the county and prefecture level coexisted in Tianjin. Both of the two temples consist of the Main South Gate (Wanren Gongqiang), Pan Pond (Pan Chi), Lingxing Gate, Dacheng Gate, Dacheng Hall, Chongsheng Ancestral Hall and Eastern and Western Side Hall, etc. Decorated with grey bricks and tiles, the County Temple (Xian Temple) is smaller compared with the Prefecture Temple (Fu Temple) whose buildings along the axis of the complex are decorated with yellow glazed tiles. In Ming, Qing Dynasties and the early period of Republic of China, Confucian Temple (Wen Temple) was the place to offer sacrifices to Confucius in spring and autumn. Now it is the Confucian Temple Museum.

府庙大成殿
Dacheng Hall of the Prefecture Temple

府庙大成门
Dacheng Gate of the Prefecture Temple

原英国俱乐部
Former Tientsin Club

英国俱乐部初建于1860年前后，也叫“英国球房”，附设“兰心戏院”，系英租界侨民集资修建。每逢天津港封冻期间，侨民们即集中在俱乐部中举行舞会、午后茶会、音乐会或戏剧演出，是当时天津租界社会的艺术中心，现为办公用房。现存建筑为1904年重建，位于和平区解放北路201号，天津市文物保护单位，特殊保护等级历史风貌建筑，占地面积约7 300m^2，建筑面积约3 000m^2。砖木结构二层楼房（设有地下室）。建筑采用对称布局，窗间墙均匀布置的爱奥尼克巨柱强调了竖向构图，丰富的立面装饰和拱券门窗，体现了典型的折中主义建筑风格。

外景 Exterior view

The club, also called the British Ballroom, was initially opened about 1860 accompanied with the Lyceum Theatre. Raised financially by the immigrants of the British Concession in Tianjin, the club served the British immigrants as an entertainment center for holding balls and pink-tea parties, as well as enjoying concerts and operas.

The preserved building was reconstructed in 1904, located at No.201 North Jiefang Road, Heping District and listed as the heritage site under city protection and the special protection historic architecture in Tianjin. The building is used as an office building nowadays, covering an area of about 7,300 square meters, and about 3,000 square meters in floor area.

The brick-wood composite construction is two-storied, with its basement. As a symmetrical design, the building attracts people's attention to its vertical structure by locating the massive Ionic columns orderly between the windows. Rich in exterior decoration and variation of the arched windows, it tastes to be typically in eclectic style.

外檐局部 Partial outer-eaves

外檐局部
Partial outer-eaves

外景 Exterior view

原德国俱乐部

Former Club Concordia

原德国俱乐部位于河西区解放南路273号，天津市文物保护单位，特殊保护等级历史风貌建筑，现为办公用房。俱乐部建于1907年，又名德国会馆或康科迪亚俱乐部，是德国侨民政治、社交和文娱活动中心。二楼走廊墙壁刻有解释“康科迪亚”含义的拉丁文：“同心同德则盛，离心离德则衰。”该建筑的占地面积约3 100 m²，建筑面积约3 500 m²，砖木结构三层坡顶楼房，门窗造型多采用拱形元素；建筑装饰丰富，细部精致，具有明显的日耳曼建筑风格。

The preserved site of the former Club Concordia was located at No.273 South Jiefang Road, Hexi District, classified in the list of the heritage site under city protection and the special protection historic architecture in Tianjin, covering an area of about 3,100 square meters, and about 3,500 square meters in floor area. The building was built in 1907. The Club Concordia, also known as the German Club, served mainly for the German immigrants as their political, social and recreational center. Some words in Latin were inscribed on the wall of the second floor, explaining the meaning of the Club: if "Concordia"—"all the people join their efforts for common purpose" will bring out prosperity; and if "discordia"—everyone only concerns oneself might lead to collapse.

The brick-wood three-storied building is designed with the sloping roofs. It tastes typically to be in Nordic style.

大厅楼梯 Stairs in the lobby

内景 Inside view

外景 Exterior view

原英国乡谊俱乐部
Former Tianjin Race Club

原英国乡谊俱乐部位于河西区马场道188号，天津市文物保护单位，特殊保护等级历史风貌建筑，现为商业用房。该建筑建于1925年，其建筑面积约为8 000 m²，英商景明工程司设计，又称“新英国俱乐部”。俱乐部包括剧场、舞厅、室内游泳池、乒乓球室、保龄球室、图书馆等多项游乐设施，是外国侨民和上流社会娱乐消遣的场所。1941年太平洋战争爆发后被日军占用，改名“国际俱乐部”；1945年日本投降后改为美军“军官俱乐部”。该建筑为混合结构庭院式二层楼房，建筑立面呈对称形式，造型稳重，红砖饰面朴素大方。内部装饰精美适用，各项娱乐功能在当时的天津首屈一指。俱乐部坐落于英国跑马场内，周围园林景观优美，具有浓郁的英国田园风格。

Standing at No.188 Machang Avenue, Hexi District, the former Tianjin Race Club is now the heritage site under city protection and the special protection historic architecture in Tianjin and is used as a business building. It was built in 1925 and has a floor area of about 8,000 square meters. As was designed by British Hemmings & Parkin Ltd., it was also known as New British Club. Equipped with theatre, dance hall, indoor swimming pool, pingpang room, bowling alley and library, the club was exclusive to foreigners and the upper crust. After the Pacific War broke out in 1941, the Japanese invaders took it over and renamed it as International Club. And after Japan's surrender in 1945, it fell into American's hand and was changed into Armed Forces Officer's Club. Featured a simple red brick facade with a perfect symmetry and beautiful interior decorations, the facilities in this two-storied building topped its kind in Tianjin at that time. Located inside the race ground in the British concession and featured a beautiful garden landscape, the building epitomized British pastoral style.

老游泳池
Old swimming pool

一楼大厅 Lobby on the first floor

外景 Exterior view

原回力球场

Former Jai alai Sportcenter

原回力球场位于河北区民族路47号，天津市区、县文物保护单位，重点保护等级历史风貌建筑，现为商业用房。回力球场由意商富马加里创办，是借回力球运动赌博的场所，内设赛场、餐厅、休息室等，是当时华北地区最大的室内游乐场。1942年，球场改由瑞士人李亚溥经营，改名为“海莱运动场”，抗日战争胜利后停业。该建筑建于1934年，占地面积约4 000 m^2，建筑面积约6 400 m^2，意大利建筑师鲍乃弟和瑞士人凯思乐设计，孟特劳克公司施工。中华人民共和国成立后，由关颂坚和凯思乐重新设计改建为“工人文化宫”。建筑为钢混结构楼房，立面设计强调竖向构图，具有现代建筑特征。角部塔楼在1976年地震中损毁，2008年恢复。

The former Jai alai Sportcenter, situated at No.47 Minzu Road, Hebei District, is now the heritage site under city/county protection and the important protection historic architecture in Tianjin and is used for business now. It was a gambling house started by V. Fumagalli and was the largest indoor sport center with sports ground, dining hall and lounge in North China. In 1942, M.Leopold, a Swiss took over the center and renamed it as Hailai Sportcenter. After the victory of Anti-Japanese War in 1945, it was closed down. The center was designed by an Italian architect Bonetti and a Swiss called Kessler and was built in 1934, covering an area of about 4,000 square meters and having a floor area of about 6,400 square meters. After the PRC was established, it was redesigned by Guan Songjian and Kessler and rebuilt into the Workers' Club. This steel-concrete structure building is very modern because of the vertical format on the facade. In the 1976 Tangshan Earthquake, the tower on the roof was damaged and was restored in 2008.

夜景 Night view

天津西客站主站房

Main House of the West Railway Station in Tianjin

天津西客站主站房位于红桥区西站前街1号，全国重点文物保护单位，特殊保护等级历史风貌建筑。天津西客站建于1910年，是津浦铁路的重要站点。清光绪三十四年（1908年）清政府开始修建（天）津浦（口）铁路，1912年全线通车。其建筑面积约1 700 m^2，砖混结构二层楼房，建筑坐北朝南，平面呈凸字形，红瓦坡顶，清水砖墙，建筑立面强调对称构图，造型丰富，窗式、窗套富于变化，属典型的折中主义建筑风格。

背立面局部
Partial back elevation

As the important heritage site under state protection and the special protection historic architecture in Tianjin, the West Railway Station sits at No.1 Front Street of the West Railway Station, Hongqiao District, and about 1,700 square meters in floor area. The station was built in 1910, serving as an important joint of the Jin–Pu (Tianjin–Pukou) railway which had initially been constructed in 1908(the 34th year of the Guangxu's Reign, Qing Dynasty) and completed in 1912. Facing southward, the two-storied brick-concrete construction has its facade look convex-shaped. It is in a symmetrical design with red-tiled sloping roof and dry brick walls, rich in structures, and windows along with their trims. The design presents typically in eclectic style.

候车厅
Lounge of the Station

外景 Exterior view

软席候车室
SOFT SEAT WAITING ROOM

外景 Exterior view

原大陆银行仓库

Warehouse of the Former Continental Bank

20世纪20年代，大陆银行为使码头仓储和抵押贷款有所保证，修建了大型仓库，存放各种商货，从而取得了外商70%的仓储业务。该建筑位于和平区张自忠路223号，特殊保护等级历史风貌建筑，建于1925年，建筑面积约为7 700 m²。其为四层（局部六层）混合结构楼房,清水砖墙，建筑体量厚重敦实，舒展大方，建筑内部设有壁垒森严的金库，现仍在使用。

A giant warehouse was set up by the Continental Bank in 1920s to further meet its operational requirements for storage and mortgage loan. 70% storage business of the foreign businessmen was obtained by the Bank therefore. Located at No.223 Zhang Zizhong Road, Heping District, the warehouse built in 1925 has been classified as the special protection historic architecture in Tianjin. It covers a floor area of about 7,700 square meters. With dry brick wall the composite structure is mainly four-storied but partially six-storied. The building looks massive and decent. It was also designed with a well-guarded treasury which is still in use nowadays.

雪景 Snow view

影壁 Screen wall

石家大院
Mansion of the Shi's Family

石家大院坐落于西青区杨柳青镇，全国重点文物保护单位，特殊保护等级历史风貌建筑，现为博物馆。石家为清代津门“八大家”之一，此宅系石家后人石元仕宅第。该建筑为典型的四合院住宅建筑群，始建于1875年。整个院落以“箭道”为中轴，分为东西两部分，共有10个独立的四合院或三合院，房屋200余间，占地面积约6 000 m^2，建筑面积约3 000 m^2，院中的戏楼是我国北方规模较大的民居戏楼。房屋均为砖木结构，屋顶皆为硬山，起人字脊或元宝脊，外墙为青砖砌筑。砖、木、石雕等建筑装饰工艺精美，造型别致，并借鉴了西方建筑装饰特色，颇具观赏价值。

The Mansion of the Shi's Family lies in the town of Yangliuqing, Xiqing District. It is listed as the important heritage site under state protection and the special protection historic architecture in Tianjin, and used as a museum now. The Shi's Family was one of the eight most celebrated families in Tianjin in the Qing Dynasty. The residence introduced here belonged to Shi Yuanshi, one of the offsprings of the Shi's Family. Built in 1875, the Mansion was a complex design in the traditional Chinese courtyard house style—enclosing dwelling block with its inner courtyard. Taking the main passage as the axis, the buildings were arranged respectively on the east and west sides along the passage. The

大门外景 Exterior view of the main gate

mansion consists of 10 blocks, some with buildings in four directions while some in three directions. There are more than 200 rooms in the mansion. It covers an area of about 6,000 square meters and its floor area is about 3,000 square meters. Moreover, even a theater is located within the residence, which is considered as one of the larger scale theaters of the civil residence in North China. All the buildings are constructed with gables roofs, as well as the herringbone and curved ridges. The wall of the buildings is made of black brick, finished with exquisite carvings of brick, wood and stone. The design of the mansion is merged with the Western architectural features, being more tasteful.

戏楼内景
Inner view of the Theater

内院门 Gateway to a courtyard

鸟瞰图 Bird's eye view

影壁 Screen wall

外景 Exterior view

徐朴庵旧宅

Former Residence of Xu Pu'an

徐朴庵旧宅位于南开区老城厢东门里大街202号，天津市文物保护单位，重点保护等级历史风貌建筑，俗称“徐家大院”，建于清末民初，现为老城博物馆。徐朴庵为英商麦加利银行买办。大院采用我国传统合院砖木结构体系，占地面积约1 400 m²，建筑面积约700 m²，建筑坐北朝南，中轴线由三进院落组成。东西两侧为箭道，是内部通道，可作紧急疏散用，具有天津地方特色。该建筑群均为中国传统民居小式做法，采用青瓦硬山屋顶，墙体采用青砖磨砖对缝，门窗为传统木雕和花饰。建筑中还装饰了大量做工精细、寓意吉祥的精美砖雕、木雕，堪称工艺杰作。

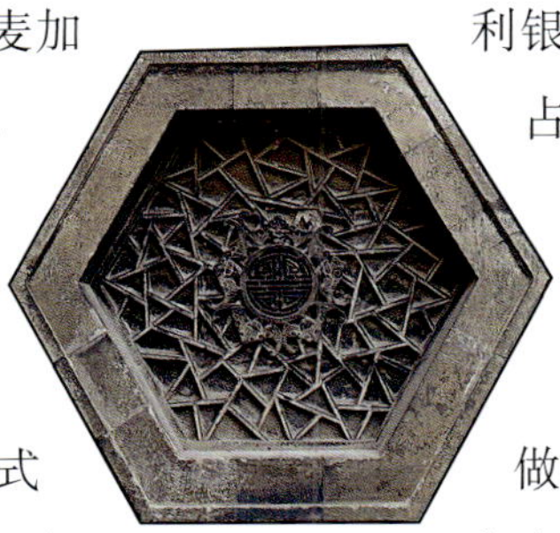

内院 Inner yard

内景 Inner view

Located at No.202 Inner Dong Men Street of Lao Cheng Xiang, Nankai District, the former Residence of Xu Pu'an is the heritage site under city protection and the important protection historic architecture. Built in the end of Qing Dynasty, it used to be called Xu's Courtyard, and now is Old Town Museum. Xu Pu'an was a comprador of Chartered Bank of England. Covering an area of about 1,400 square meters, the courtyard applied traditional Chinese brick-wood structure. With a floor area of about 700 square meters, it faces south, the axis is constituted by three independent courtyards. On both east and west sides there are arrow roads which are internal corridors used for emergency evacuation. It is of typical local feature. The groups of buildings are all traditional Chinese small-type residence including black-tile gable roof and grinding bricks jointing walls, doors and windows with wood carving and floral decoration. A great deal of fine brick sculptures and wooden sculptures with auspicious connotations and superior workmanship decorate the building, which is considered as a masterwork of architecture.

夜景 Night view

通庆里
Tongqing Lane

通庆里位于南开区古文化街北端东侧，天津市重点保护等级历史风貌建筑，现为商业用房。通庆里建于清末民初，占地面积约1 800 m²，建筑面积约2 100 m²，为六个独立的院落串联组成的里巷。每个院落内相对有两座青砖二层楼房，砖木结构，坡屋顶，首层及二层均建有开敞外廊。建筑功能、风格、装饰和里巷布局既有中国传统建筑元素，又有西洋建筑符号，融合了中国南北方民居的风格，集萃了东西方建筑符号，是天津近代折中主义建筑的代表。

Located at the east side of the north end of Ancient Culture Street of Nankai District, Tongqing Lane is an important protection historic architecture and commercial real estate now. Built in the end of Qing Dynasty, it covers an area of about 1,800 square meters with a floor area of about 2,100 square meters. It is a lane constituted by six independent courtyards.There are two two-storied black-brick buildings facing each other in each courtyard, which have a brick-wood structure and sloping roofs. Open verandas are set on both stories. Traditional Chinese and Western architectural elements can be found out in architectural function, style, decorations and the layout of the lane. The residential styles of both north China and south China are combined while both oriental and Western architectural symbols are gathered, which makes the lane a representative of eclectic architecture in modern history of Tianjin.

内院 Inner yard

外景 Exterior view

盛装开街
游客服务中心
通慶里
晟藝閣

主楼外景
Exterior view of the Main Building

静　园
Jingyuan Garden

静园位于和平区鞍山道70号，天津市文物保护单位，特殊保护等级历史风貌建筑，占地面积约3 000 m^2，建筑面积约1 900 m^2。静园原名乾园，为北洋政府驻日公使陆宗舆私邸，建于1921年。该建筑由主楼、图书馆、佣人房、厨房、车库组成。主楼为砖木结构二层楼房，局部三层。一楼为客厅、餐厅，二楼为卧室。室内为木楼梯、木地板；外檐为混水墙面，局部硫缸砖清水砖墙。建筑为多坡屋顶，红瓦屋面，各建筑之间由连廊相连，具有折中主义建筑特征。1929年末代皇帝溥仪迁居乾园，将“乾园”改名“静园”，取“静以养吾浩然之气”之意。1931年溥仪由此出逃到大连，后当上伪满洲国的傀儡“皇帝”。

天津解放后，静园曾作为办公用房，后成为多户居民居住的大杂院。2005年10月，天津市国土资源和房屋管理局依据《天津市历史风貌建筑保护条例》对静园内45户居民进行了腾迁，拆除了院内的违章建筑，依照“修旧如故、安全适用”的原则，对静园进行复原整修。2007年7月，复原整修工程全部竣工，静园对社会开放。

Constructed in 1921, Jingyuan Garden is located at No.70 Anshan Avenue, Heping District, listed as the heritage site under city protection and the important historic architecture under special protection in Tianjin. It covers an area of about 3,000 square meters, and its floor area is about 1,900 square meters. Originally named Qianyuan Garden, it was the private residence

西跨院
Western yard

夜景 Night view

of Lu Zongyu, minister-counselor to Japan appointed by the Beiyang Warlords' Government. The complex consists of the main building, library, servants' chamber, kitchen and garage. The main brick-wood building is mainly two-storied while three-storied partially. The first floor serves as a living room and a dinning room, while the second floor as bedrooms. The stairways and floors are made of wood inside the building. The exterior walls are mainly stucco-finished but partially dried with glazed quarry tiles. With red-tiled sloping-roofs, all the buildings in the garden are linked by corridors. The whole complex looks typically eclectic.

Then in 1929, Qianyuan Garden was changed to Jingyuan Garden by Puyi, the last emperor of Qing Dynasty, when he settled here. "Jing"means"stillness", and the garden was named after it in hint that

the abdicated emperor would like to strengthen himself with noble spirit in a moveless environment. It was also from here that Puyi escaped to Dalian in 1931 and took the "crown" again. After the liberation of Tianjin, Jingyuan Garden was used as an office building and then as a civil dwelling for many households. Well in October of 2005, the 45 households were arranged to move out of the garden and the unapproved structure not belonging to the original complex was demolished by the Land Resources and Housing Administration, Tianjin via the *Regulations on the Protection of Building of Historic Significance, Tianjin*. Restoration and renovation were initiated in line with the principle of "Restoring to its Original State and guaranteeing Safety and Applicability". And by July of 2007, the work had been completed and the garden had reopened to the public.

书房 Study room

客厅 Living room

三楼楼梯间 Stair hall on the third floor

外景 Exterior view

张　园

Former Residence of Mr. Zhang

张园位于和平区鞍山道59号，天津市文物保护单位，重点保护等级历史风貌建筑，原是晚清武举张彪私邸，现为办公用房。张彪（1860—1927），字虎臣，山西榆次人，出身武举，赐总兵衔，曾任湖北营务处总办、标统、提督，后任驻武昌陆军第六镇统制。武昌起义爆发后，携眷逃往日本。1916年在天津原日租界建私宅“张园”寓居。1924年12月，孙中山先生赴京途中，曾下榻于此。末代皇帝溥仪被驱逐出宫后，于1925年来到天津，在此居住至1929年，而后迁居静园。“七七事变”后，张园被日本驻屯军占用并进行重建，作为驻屯军军官的官邸。

现存建筑为混合结构二层楼房（设有地下室），占地面积约6 700 m^2，建筑面积约3 300 m^2，建筑布局不对称，转角处设有塔楼，强调竖向构图。建筑借鉴意大利古典复兴造型，采用拱券窗、拱券入口门厅、高耸的塔楼等建筑元素，红瓦坡顶，清水砖墙，使得立面效果丰富、热烈；内部装修考究，细部设计丰富。

Located at No.59 Anshan Avenue, Heping District, the former Residence of Mr. Zhang is the heritage site under city protection and the important protection historic architecture. Formerly a private residence of Zhang Biao, a successful military candidate in the imperial provincial examination in late Qing Dynasty, it is presently an office building. Zhang Biao (1860–1927), with a courtesy name of Huchen, was born in Yuci, Shanxi Province. He was a successful military candidate in the imperial provincial examination and was granted a title of Garrison Commander. He was once the director of Hubei Troop Affairs Office, regimental commander, provincial commander-in-chief and then commander of the Sixth Army Division in Wuchang. After the outbreak of Wuchang Uprising, he carried his family members to flee to Japan. In 1916, he started to build his private residence “Zhangyuan Garden”

内景 Inner view

in the Japanese concession in Tianjin. Mr. Sun Yat-sen had stayed here on his way to Peking in December 1924. The last emperor, Pu Yi, came to Tianjin in 1925 after being expelled from the Royal Palace and lived in the place till moving to Jingyuan Garden in 1929. After the July 7th Incident, Zhangyuan Garden was occupied by Japanese garrison army and reconstructed as a mansion for garrison army officers.

The existing construction is a two-storied building in mixed structure (with basements), covering an area of about 6,700 square meters and a floor area of about 3,300 square meters. The architectural composition is asymmetric with towers at corners and a focus on vertical composition. The building borrowed the Italian classical revival modeling and adopted architectural elements such as arch windows, arch entrance halls and steep towers. With red tiled sloping roofs and fair-faced walls, the building shows rich and strong facade effects. The interior decoration is carefully selected and the design of details is abundant.

外景 Exterior view

段祺瑞旧宅

Former Residence of Duan Qirui

段祺瑞旧宅位于和平区鞍山道38号，天津市文物保护单位，重点保护等级历史风貌建筑，现为办公用房。段祺瑞（1865—1936），字芝泉，安徽合肥人，皖系军阀首领。1885年段祺瑞考入天津武备学堂炮科，1889年毕业后赴德国军事院校学习炮兵科，并在克虏伯炮厂实习。1890年回国后，他先后在北洋军械局和随营武备学堂任职。1896年任小站新建陆军炮兵学堂总办兼炮兵第三营统带，与王士珍、冯国璋并称“北洋三杰”。辛亥革命后，他曾任民国政府陆军总长、国务总理，在1920年的直皖战争中被击败下台，寓居天津。1924年第二次直奉战争后，直系军阀失败，段祺瑞重掌大权，就任“中华民国临时执政”；1926年被冯玉祥驱逐，再次寓居天津，1933年移居上海。

该建筑建于1920年，占地面积约3 200 m^2，建筑面积约3 100 m^2，为混合结构的三层楼房（设有地下室）。建筑布局以西方生活方式为参考，首层为起居、会客、舞厅、餐厅等公共空间，二、三层为卧室等私密空间。建筑造型为对称的古典复兴式，混水墙面，一、二层均设有开敞柱廊，采用简易古罗马柱式，入口处设有条石高台阶，建筑庄严气派。

外景 Exterior view

Located at No.38 Anshan Avenue, Heping District, the Former Residence of Duan Qirui is the heritage site under city protection and the important protection historic architecture and is currently used as an office building. Duan Qirui (1865–1936), with a courtesy name of Zhiquan and born in Hefei, Anhui Province, was the leader of the Wan Xi warlords. In 1885, he passed the examination and entered into the Artillery Department of Tianjin Military School. After his graduation in 1889, he was sent to a Germany military college to study artillery and practiced in Krupp Works. After returning to China in 1890, he took office in the Beiyang Armory and the Military Staff Academy successively. In 1896, he was named as the director of the Artillery Academy of the New Army in Xiaozhan and the artillery commander. He was known as one of the "Three Outstanding Persons of Beiyang", including Wang Shizhen and Feng Guozhang. After the Revolution of 1911, he was named as the minister of war and then the premier in the government of the Republic of China. He was defeated and forced to step down during the Zhili-Anhui War in 1920, then he moved to Tianjin and lived there. When the Zhi Xi failed in the second Zhili-Fengtian War in 1924, Duan Qirui regained the power and took the post of "Temporary Chief Executive of the Republic of China". He was exiled by Feng Yuxiang in 1926 and lived in Tianjin again, then moved to Shanghai in 1933.

Built in 1920, the three-storied building (with basements) in mixed structure covers an area of about 3,200 square meters and a floor area of about 3,100 square meters. The architectural composition is in a Western living style: the first floor consists of common spaces for sitting, reception, dancing and dinning, etc.; the second and third floors are private spaces such as bedrooms. The architectural modeling is a symmetrical classic revival: furred walls, open porticos supported by simple ancient Roman columns in the first and second floors, high steps paved by block stones at the entrance, all presenting solemnity and magnificence.

楼梯 Stairs

二层内景 Inner view of the second floor

主入口内景
Inner view of the main entrance

袁氏旧宅

Former Residence of the Yuan's Family

袁氏旧宅位于河北区海河东路39号，天津市文物保护单位，特殊保护等级历史风貌建筑，现为商业用房。这是袁世凯族侄袁乃宽为袁世凯督建的住宅，但住宅未完工，袁世凯已暴死。袁乃宽（1868—？），河南项城人，曾参与袁世凯复辟帝制活动，一度出任农商总长，去职后寓居天津。

该建筑建于1918年，占地面积约1 800 m^2，建筑面积约2 100 m^2，主楼为混合结构三层楼房（附楼二层），红瓦坡顶，混水墙面。建筑造型独特，装饰繁多，有荷兰滨水建筑特征；中部的六角形塔楼成为构图中心；建筑室内设隐身处和逃生处，逃生暗道上达屋顶露台，下通海河，布局独特；面向海河设八角形观景房和风水窗，可观四时风景，寓意吉祥。

外景 Exterior view

楼梯 Stairs

The former Residence of Yuan Shikai, which is now used as a commercial building, is located at No.39 East Haihe Road, Hebei District, classified as the heritage site under city protection and the special protection historic architecture in Tianjin. The residence was built under the supervision of Yuan Naikuan(1868–?), nephew of Yuan Shikai. It was originally for Yuan Shikai, but he died before its completion. Born in Xiangcheng County of Henan Province, Yuan Naikuan had been the supporter for his uncle to restore the monarchy and served once the Minister of Agriculture and Commerce. He moved to settle in Tianjin after his retirement. The resident was built in 1918. It covers an area of about 1,800 square meters, and its floor area is about 2,100 square meters. With its red-tiled sloping roofs and stucco finished walls, the main building of the residence is a composite three-storied structure while the Annex being two-storied. It is characterized as the architecture of the waterfront considering its unique style and rich decorations. A hexagon towered section serves as the central point of the building. Moreover the secret room and safety passage were designed in the building. Especially the safety passage was leading its way up to the terrace on the roof and down to the Haihe River at a distance. Facing the river, the octagon room was designed purposely with landscape windows for people to enjoy the views along with lucks all the year round.

外檐局部 Partial outer-eaves

外景 Exterior view

冯国璋旧宅

Former Residence of Feng Guozhang

冯国璋旧宅位于河北区民主道50～54号，天津市文物保护单位，特殊保护等级历史风貌建筑，现为办公用房。冯国璋（1857—1919），字华甫，河北河间人，直系军阀首领，毕业于天津武备学堂。辛亥革命后出任直隶都督、江苏都督。1916年他当选为副总统；1917年任代理大总统；1918年去职，寓居天津、北京，曾在天津投资金融、工业、矿业及房地产。

该建筑建于1912年，占地面积约700 m²，建筑面积约1 900 m²，由奥地利建筑师布吕纳设计建造。建筑为砖木结构二层楼房，呈对称布局，中央盔顶部分为视觉中心，两端三角山花又加强了这种构图形式。建筑体量适宜、舒展，色彩搭配协调统一。

Located at No.50~54 Minzhu Avenue of Hebei District, the former Residence of Feng Guozhang is the heritage site under city protection and the special protection historic architecture, and now used as an office building. Feng Guozhang (1857–1919), with a courtesy name Huafu, born in Hejian of Hebei Province, was the head of Zhi Xi warlord. He graduated from Tianjin Military School, and served as the governor of Zhili and Jiangsu Provinces after the Revolution of 1911. In 1916, he was elected the Vice President of the Republic of China. In 1917, he was the acting President. In 1918, he left the post and lived in Tianjin and Beijing. He used to invest in finance, industry, mining and real estate. Built in 1912, his former residence covers an area of 700 square meters and a floor area of 1,900 square meters. Designed by an Austrian architect, it is a two-storied brick-timber structure. The layout is bilaterally symmetrical with the central top as the visual center. The triangle pediments on both sides enforce the symmetry. The building has a proper size which harmonizes well with the color collocation.

饮冰室外景 Exterior view of Yinbingshi

梁启超旧宅

Former Residence of Liang Qichao

梁启超旧宅、“饮冰室”书斋位于河北区民族路44～46号，占地面积约2 500 m²，全国重点文物保护单位，重点保护等级历史风貌建筑，现为纪念馆。梁启超（1873—1929），广东新会人，中国近代著名思想家和学者，清末与康有为共同发动“公车上书”，主张维新。辛亥革命后他先后出任司法总长、财政部长等职，1915年定居天津。他反对袁世凯称帝，并与云南督军蔡锷在天津共同策划反袁武装起义，在五四运动中倡导“诗界革命”“小说革命”和白话文。

其旧宅位于河北区民族路44号，建于1914年，建筑面积约1 000 m²，砖木结构二层楼房（设有地下室），设有开敞柱廊，东侧转角处的八角形角楼成为最主要的竖向构图。“饮冰室”书斋位于民族路46号，建于1924年，建筑面积约900 m²，由意大利建筑师白罗尼欧设计，砖木结构二层楼房（设有地下室）。建筑平面布局为“凹”字形，强调对称构图，装饰较多且造型复杂，体量厚重敦实，带有古典主义色彩。

雪景 Snow view

饮冰室客厅 Living room of Yinbingshi

Being the important heritage site under state protection and the important protection historic architecture in Tianjin, the former Residence of Liang Qichao and his studio-Yinbingshi, are located respectively at No.44~46 Minzu Road, Heibei District, and cover an area of about 2,500 square meters. The site is a museum nowadays. Born in Xinhui County of Guangdong Province, Liang Qichao (1873–1929) is regarded as one of the most famous ideologists and scholars in modern China. It was he who submitted the Joint Petition of Imperial Examination Candidates to the Emperor along with Kang Youwei, calling for the social reform in China. After the Revolution of 1911, he was appointed as the minister of Judiciary and Finance, etc. one after another. He moved to settle in Tianjin in 1915. He fought against the restoration of monarchy by Yuan Shikai and further planned to launch an anti-Yuan uprising with general Cai E, Military Governor of Yunnan Province. He also made his efforts to bring the reformations to the areas of poetry, novel and language.

The former Residence of Liang Qichao was built in 1924, at 44 Minzu Road, and its floor area is about 1,000 square meters. The brick-wood building is two-storied along with its basement and open colonnade. The octagonal pavilion at the east corner serves as the major vertical structure of the architecture. Designed by Bironio, an Italian architect, and his Studio at 46 Minzu Road, Yinbingshi, was constructed in 1924, and its floor area is about 900 square meters. This brick-wood structure is composed in a symmetrically concave plan, rich in shapes and decorations and with the basement as well. It looks massive and steady, presenting with classicism.

饮冰室内景 Inner view of Yinbingshi

汤玉麟旧宅

Former Residence of Tang Yulin

汤玉麟旧宅位于河北区民主道40号，天津市文物保护单位，重点保护等级历史风貌建筑，占地面积约2 600 m^2，建筑面积约3 200 m^2为北洋政府交通总长吴毓麟于1922年建造的私宅，后卖与汤玉麟。汤玉麟（1871—1949），山东人，出身绿林，曾任热河省政府主席兼第三十六师师长，去职后寓居天津。该建筑为混合结构二层楼房，红瓦坡顶，平面布局严谨对称，立面装饰丰富，做工精美，开窗形式多样，具有折中主义建筑特征。

外景 Exterior view

As the heritage site under city protection and the important protection historic architecture in Tianjin, the former Residence of Tang Yulin sits at No.40 Minzhu Avenue, Hebei District. It covers an area of about 2,600 square meters, and a floor area of about 3,200 square meters. It was originally built in 1922 by Wu Yulin, Minister of Communications for the Beiyang Warlord Government and then purchased by Tang Yulin in 1930 as his resident.

Tang Yulin (1871—1949) came from Shandong Province, once being a bandit and then the commander of the 36th Division and even the governor of Rehe Province. He settled in Tianjin after his retirement.

This composite structure is two-storied with red-tiled sloping roofs. It was laid out in a strictly symmetrical style. Rich in ornaments under the outer-eaves and with windows in different shapes, the architecture tastes delicate and presents with an eclectic atmosphere.

外檐细部
Details of the outer-eaves

鲍贵卿旧宅

Former Residence of Bao Guiqing

鲍贵卿旧宅位于河北区平安街81号，天津市区、县文物保护单位，重点保护等级历史风貌建筑，现为办公用房。鲍贵卿（1866—1934），字霆九，辽宁海城人，天津北洋武备学堂工程科毕业，曾任北洋政府陆军总长、黑龙江督军、吉林督军等职，下野后寓居天津。他于1920—1921年购得此楼并改建成一座豪华的花园住宅。

该建筑为混合结构二层楼房，局部三层，带地下室，多坡瓦屋顶。外檐为青砖清水墙面。一、二层设柱廊，三层局部退台形成大露台，露台上建有三个风格迥异的亭子，中间为带有罗曼式屋顶和简化科林斯柱式的西洋凉亭，东面为中国传统的圆攒尖亭，西面为较简洁的西洋凉亭，室内装饰豪华。中西合璧的建筑设计，印证了当时天津中西文化交融的情况。

外景 Exterior view

楼梯 Stairs

内檐门 Gate under the inner-eaves

精美的木雕 Exquisite wood-carvings

Located at No.81 Ping'an Street of Hebei District, the former Residence of Bao Guiqing is the heritage site under city/county protection and the important protection historic architecture and now used as an office building. Bao Guiqing (1866-1934), with a courtesy name Tingjiu, was born in Haicheng, Liaoning Province and graduated from Tianjin Beiyang Military School, majoring in engineering. He used to be the Chief of Army in the Beiyang Warlord Government, warlord of Heilongjiang Province and Jilin Province. He lived in Tianjin after falling out of power. He purchased the building from 1920 to 1921 and renovated it into a luxurious garden house.

It is a two-storied and partially three-storied mixed structure with a basement and multi-tile sloping roofs. The external is fair-faced black-bricked wall. Colonnades are set on the first and second floors. On the third floor there is a big balcony with three pavilions which are different in style. In the middle is a Western pavilion with a Roman roof and simplified Corinthian columns. On the east is a traditional Chinese pavilion with a conical roof while on the west is a simple western pavilion. Inside the house there are luxurious decorations. The architectural design is an evidence of the combination of Chinese and Western cultures in Tianjin then.

外景 Exterior view

曹禺故居纪念馆

许氏旧宅

Former Residence of Xu's Family

许氏旧宅位于和平区睦南道11号，全国重点文物保护单位，重点保护等级历史风貌建筑，现为办公用房，奉系军阀张作霖的四夫人许氏曾在此居住。

该建筑建于1926年，占地面积约2 300 m^2，建筑面积约1 000 m^2，由奥地利建筑师盖苓设计。建筑为三层砖木结构，采用英国维多利亚时期民居建筑形式，平面布局合理，使用功能齐全。红瓦坡顶，清水红砖墙面。立面构图简洁大方，特点鲜明，高耸的坡屋顶与外露木屋架，使建筑显得亲切朴素。

Located at No.11 Munan Avenue, Heping District, the former residence of Xu's family is the important heritage site under state protection and the important protection historic architecture and used as an office building now. The fourth wife of Zhang Zuolin, a Feng Xi warlord, once lived here.

Designed by an Austrian architect named Geyling, the building was constructed in 1926, covering an area of about 2,300 square meters and a floor area of about 1,000 square meters. It adopted three-storied brick-timber structure, applying an architectural form of folk residence in the British Victorian period. The floor layout is reasonable, and the functions of use is complete. The sloping roofs are red-tiled, and the walls are fair-faced with red bricks. The facade composition is concise and elegant with distinguished and outstanding features. The steep sloping roofs and the exposed wood framework make the building amiable

一楼大厅
Lobby on the first floor

张勋旧宅

Former Residence of Zhang Xun

张勋旧宅位于河西区浦口道6号，天津市文物保护单位，重点保护等级历史风貌建筑，现为办公用房。张勋（1854—1923），江西人，行伍出身，积功至参将；1895年参加小站练兵，任工兵营管带，后升至总兵。1902年他奉调至北京，守卫紫禁城端门，嗣后擢为云南提督、甘肃提督、江南提督、江苏巡抚兼署理两江总督、南洋大臣。辛亥革命后，张勋表示仍效忠清室，所部一律保留辫发，他遂有“辫帅”之称，曾任江苏督军、长江巡阅使。1917年张勋利用大总统黎元洪与国务卿段祺瑞的“府院之争”，以“调解”为名，率军进入北京，拥戴溥仪复辟，自封为议政大臣、直隶总督兼北洋大臣。复辟失败后，他寓居天津，曾被任为热河林垦督办，但未就职。他在天津他曾投资金融业，并建有大片房产。

旧宅为两幢独立的二层砖木结构的楼房，建于20世纪初，占地面积约为15 100 m^2，建筑面积约5 100 m^2，由德国工程师考特、鲁斯·凯甘尔设计。红瓦坡顶，混水墙面，室内装修考究。两楼以开敞柱廊相连接，建筑体量轻盈，色彩搭配协调。

2号楼外景 Exterior view of No.2 Building

楼梯与穿衣镜
Staircase and the pier glass

The former Residence of Zhang Xun is located at No.6 Pukou Avenue, Hexi District. It has been classified as the heritage site under city protection and the important protection historic architecture in Tianjin. It covers an area of about 15,100 square meters and its floor area is about 5,100 square meters, used as an office building now. Zhang Xun (1854–1923), born in Jiangxi Province, rose from the ranks and was promoted to assistant general. He participated in the Xiaozhan troop-training in 1895 and was appointed captain of engineer battalion, later promoted to garrison commander. He was transferred under an order to Beijing in 1902, in charge of guarding the end door of the Forbidden City. Thereafter, he was promoted to provincial commander-in-chief in Yunnan, Gansu and Jiangnan, grand coordinators of Jiangsu and Deputy Viceroy of Jiangxi and Jiangnan, later Nanyang Minister. After the Revolution of 1911, he was once appointed as the Military Governor of Jiangsu Province and the special envoy governing the Yangtze Area. However, he persisted in giving his allegiance to the Qing royalty and had his army keep their Qing hairstyle, thus being named "Pigtail General". By making use of the "Controversy between Presidential Palace and State Council" of President Li Yuanhong and Secretary of State Duan Qirui, Zhang Xun led his army into Beijing in the name of "mediation" in 1917 and supported Puyi to restore his power, titled himself Grand Councilor, Viceroy of Zhili and Beiyang Minister. He lived in Tianjin after the defeat and was appointed superintendent for forestry and land reclamation in Rehe, but he didn't take the office. He invested in banking business in Tianjin and constructed many buildings.

Built in early 1900s, the residence was designed by Germany architects Cort and Ruth Kigel, consisted of two separate brick-wood buildings, both being two-storied with red-tiled sloping roofs and stucco finished walls. A range of open colonnade was used to join the two constructions. The design presents the residence with lightness and exquisitness as well as the harmony between the colors.

外景 Exterior view

利华大楼
Leopold Building

利华大楼位于和平区解放北路116号，天津市文物保护单位，特殊保护等级历史风貌建筑，建于1939年，占地面积约2 100 m²，建筑面积约6 200 m²，由法商永和营造公司工程师穆乐设计、比利时籍犹太人李亚溥（1902—？）投资兴建，是一座办公兼住宅的公寓式大楼，也是天津最早的具有现代技术和功能的高层建筑之一。该建筑主楼十层，高43 m，钢筋混凝土框架结构，主楼外墙面采用深棕色麻面砖贴面，色彩稳重大方。建筑内部设两部电梯，布局合理。建筑构图采用非对称式，外部造型错落有致，属典型的现代主义风格。

Listed as the heritage site under city protection and the special protection historic architecture in Tianjin, the Leopold Building is located at No.116 North Jiefang Road, Heping District. It covers an area of about 2,100 square meters, and a floor area of about 6,200 square meters.

Invested by Marcel Leopold(1902—?), a Belgian Jewish, the Leopold Building was designed by Mr. P. Muller, an architect from a French engineering company—Hunke & Muller. Being an apartment-styled block, the Leopold Building was constructed in 1939 and served both for business and resident. It is considered as one of the earliest tall buildings with multifunction and modern technique in Tianjin at that time.

The main section of the Leopold Building is ten-storied with 43 meters high and in reinforced concrete structure. The walls were faced with black-brown pockmark tiles, looking more magnificent and elegant. Two elevators were adapted in the structure. It is classified as a modern nonsymmetrical design considering its sections with different heights.

外檐局部
Partial outer-eaves

鸟瞰图 Bird's eye view

外景 Exterior view

李吉甫旧宅

Former Residence of Li Jifu

李吉甫旧宅位于和平区花园路12号，天津市文物保护单位，特殊保护等级历史风貌建筑，现为办公用房。李吉甫（?—1927），天津人，英商仁记洋行买办。李氏家族是天津本帮（北帮）买办的典型代表，世称“仁记李”。“仁记李”第一代李辅臣（?—1910），曾在天津仁记洋行当佣工，因识别白银成色且善经营，被提升为会计司事，1895年升任该行帮办、买办。为方便农畜产品出口，仁记在全国各地设有仓库，就地加工羊毛、驼绒、皮张，以及猪鬃、马尾、棉花、青麻、桃仁、杏仁、草帽辫等，几至包揽了原产地的收购，以此称雄天津出口市场。李辅臣死后，仁记买办一职由其子李吉甫充任，李吉甫死后由其弟李志年接办。父子相继三十余年，积累大量财富，曾投资房地产，在英法租界广置楼房和豪宅。

该建筑建于1918年，占地面积约5 400 m^2，建筑面积约4 400 m^2，由乐利工程司瑞士建筑师陆甫设计，砖木结构二层楼房（设有地下室），是中式四合院布局的西洋建筑楼群，由两组由回廊相连的楼房构成，回廊由二十根塔什干式柱支撑。建筑造型对称稳重，立面变化丰富，室内外细部以古典雕饰为主，造型各异。

The former Residence of Li Jifu is located at No.12 Huayuan Road, Heping District, listed as the heritage site under city protection and the important protection historic architecture in Tianjin and used as an office building nowadays. Born in Tianjin, Li Jifu (?–1927) served as a comprador for the Gibb Livingston & Co., a British business. Li's family was a typical representative of local Tianjin (Northern Faction) compradors, popularly named "Renji Li". The first generation of "Renji Li" was Li Fuchen (?–1910), who had worked in Gibb Livingston & Co., (Tianjin). Thanks for the capacity of identifying the fineness of silver and good management, he was promoted to chief accountant and then assistant-in-managing as well as comprador for the company after 1895. To facilitate the export of agricultural and animal products, he set up branches and warehouses in many places across the country and processed wool, camel wool, animal skin, hog bristle, horsetail, cotton, abutilon, peach seeds, almonds and straw plaits etc. He even monopolized the purchase in the origin, thus making him renowned in Tianjin's export market. After the death of Li Fuchen, comprador of Gibb Livingston & Co., was succeeded by his son Li Jifu, and then Li Zhinian after the death of Li Jifu, his younger brother. The father and sons took the position for over 30 years and accumulated large fortune. They invested in real estates, buying many buildings and luxurious houses in the British and French concessions.

Designed by Loup, a Swiss architect, the building was built in 1918, covering an area of about 5,400 square meters and its floor area was about 2,100 square meters. The brick-wood architecture is two-storied with a basement. The residence is made up of two Western building complexes, but arranging a Chinese traditional courtyard. The two complexes are joined with a cloister formed by 20 columns of the Tuscan order. The architecture is a symmetrical design, tasting more massive and steady. Rich in variation of the elevations, sorts of classical carvings are adopted to decorate the details both inside and outside.

外景 Exterior view

外景 Exterior view

章瑞庭旧宅

Former Residence of Zhang Ruiting

章瑞庭旧宅位于和平区花园路9号，天津市文物保护单位，重点保护等级历史风貌建筑，现为天津市工商业联合会。章瑞庭（1878—1944），天津人，著名实业家。因得小站练兵军官资助，他开办了恒记德军衣庄，专为小站供应军需，继而为各派系军阀承办军衣，如东北军服装即全由恒记德承做。章瑞庭后以雄厚的资金，开办恒源帆布工厂、恒源纺织股份有限公司，并接办北洋纱厂。他曾资助南开学校教育基金十万元，该校礼堂特命名为“瑞庭礼堂”。

该建筑建于1922年，占地面积约为2 500 m²，建筑面积约2 300 m²，由奥地利建筑师盖苓设计，砖木结构三层楼房（设有地下室和阁楼），混水墙面。首层前廊入口处为半圆形花厅，上设透明玻璃顶，玻璃窗采用彩色玻璃拼镶成风景图画，厅内设喷水池，设施豪华；屋顶为红色盂莎式，造型独特，外形虚实对比；外檐的古典柱式和宝瓶栏杆精美得当，具有古典主义建筑特征。

The former Residence of Zhang Ruiting was built at No.9 Huayuan Road, Heping District, listed as the heritage site under city protection and the important protection historic architecture in Tianjin and now is Tianjin Federation of Industry and Commerce. Born in Tianjin and being a quite famous industrialist, Zhang Ruiting(1878–1944) was well-known as the founder of several enterprises one after another. Funded by the officers of training troops in Xiaozhan, he founded Hengjide Military Uniform Store to provide military supplies for Xiaozhan troops, and then the store was assigned to provide military uniforms for each

彩色玻璃窗
Stained glass window

clique, for instance, the uniforms of Northeast Army were all made by Hengjide. Afterwards, he set up Hengyuan Canvas Plant and Hengyuan Textile Co., Ltd. with abundant funds. Beiyang Cotton Mill was even taken over by him. He had subsidized 100,000 Yuan as educational fund to Naikai School, the auditorium of which was named after him.

Designed by the Austrian architect Rolf Geyling, the building was built in 1922. With the stucco finished walls, basement and attic, the brick-wood building is three-storied, while it covers an area of about 2,500 square meters and its floor area is about 2,300 square meters. A glass roofed structure in shape of a semicircle serves as the entrance hall (known as the floral hall), which is luxurious because of its elegant decorations and the fountain inside as well as its stained glass windows. The Mansard roofs and columniation combined with balusters at the outer-eaves provide the architecture with a typically classical atmosphere.

内景 Inner view

主入口 Main entrance

庆王府

Former Residence of Prince Qing

庆王府位于和平区重庆道55号，全国重点文物保护单位，特殊保护等级历史风貌建筑。该建筑于1922年由清宫内监小德张所建，1926年，清庆亲王载振购得此楼并居住，俗称“庆王府”。载振（1876—1947），清世袭庆亲王，初袭镇国将军，后加封贝子衔。1902年他任专使大臣，贺英皇加冕，并应邀访问比、法、美、日四国；1906年任农工商部尚书。1907年载振奉派赴东三省查办事件，路经天津，天津南段巡警局总办段芝贵买女伶杨翠喜送其为妾，得升任黑龙江巡抚。不久此事为御史赵启霖揭发参奏，清廷派员调查，以“查无实据”不了了之，事后载振辞去一切职务。居津期间，他投资买办高星桥新业公司兴建的劝业场、交通旅馆等实业项目，用以维持生活开销。

该建筑占地面积约4 700 m^2，建筑面积约5 000 m^2，砖木结构二层（设有地下室）内天井围合式建筑；两层外檐均设通敞柱廊，建筑形体简洁明快。室内设有共享大厅，大气、开敞，适应当时的西化生活。水刷石墙面与中国传统琉璃栏杆交相辉映，门窗玻璃上比利时工艺雕琢的中国传统花鸟栩栩如生。该建筑是当时中西合璧的典型。

一楼侧厅
Side Hall on the first floor

门厅木隔扇 Wood partition door

Classified as the important heritage site under state protection and the special protection historic architecture in Tianjin, the Former Residence of Prince Qing stands at No. 55 Chongqing Avenue, Heping District. It was built in 1922 by Zhang Lande (called Xiaodezhang more porpularly), a eunuch of the Qing Dynasty. And then in 1926, the Prince Qing of the Qing Dynasty, Zai Zhen, purchased it as his dwelling. Therefore the building has been called Palace of Prince Qing. Zai Zhen (1876–1947), hereditary Prince Qing of Qing Dynasty, initially Zhen Guo General and later ensealed the rank of Beizi. In 1902, he was appointed special envoy minister to congratulate the crowning of the British King and visited Belgium, France, U.S.A. and Japan on invitations. He was appointed as the Minister of the Department of Agriculture, Industry and Commerce in 1906. In the next year, he was ordered to investigate and deal with the events in the three Northeast provinces. When he passed Tianjin, Duan Zhigui, the director of Patrolmen Station in southern section of Tianjin, bought an actress named Yang Cuixi and sent him as a concubine. Duan Zhigui was promoted the governor of Heilongjiang Province. After a short while, the issue was disclosed by the censor Zhao Qilin. The imperial court assigned an official to investigate and ended it up with nothing definite in the reason of no actual evidence. Thereafter, Zai Zhen resigned all positions. During his stay in Tianjin, he invested in some industrial projects including Quanyechang Mall, a department store established by Xinye Company which was owned by comprador Gao Xingqiao and Communication Hotel for his expenditures of living.

Covering an area of about 4,700 square meters and with a floor area of about 5,000 square meters, the architecture was laid out in an enclosing form with a courtyard inside. With the basement, this brick-wood structure is two-storied and has got two ranges of the open colonnades respectively for both layers. The design is simple but tasteful. The shared lobby in the building is giant and elegant, suitable for the Western life-style at time. The traditional Chinese glazed balusters take the granitic stucco walls as their background and the classical Chinese flower-bird figures made of the Belgian glass seem lifelike. The Chinese and Western cultures have been mingled with each other by the design.

外景 Exterior view

内景 Inner view

外檐侧入口 Side entrance under the outer-eaves

张学铭旧宅

Former Residence of Zhang Xueming

张学铭旧宅位于和平区睦南道50号，全国重点文物保护单位，特殊保护等级历史风貌建筑，现为办公用房。张学铭（1908—1983），辽宁海城人，奉系军阀张作霖之子，著名爱国将领张学良之二弟。1928年，张学铭进入日本陆军步兵学校学习，1929年回国就职于东北军。1930年他但任天津市公安局局长，1931年4月任天津市市长兼公安局长。在任期间，张学铭严格警务、警纪，增加警务设施，半年的整训使天津警察成为了全国的模范。1931年3月，新任沈阳市公安局局长黄显生，特从天津借调警察赴沈阳警察局做示范。1931年在张学铭领导下，天津军警两次挫败了日本便衣队的暴乱活动。中华人民共和国成立后，张学铭先后任中国国民党革命委员会天津市副主委、全国政协委员、天津市政协常委。

该建筑建于1925年，占地面积约1 800 m^2，建筑面积约1 700 m^2，砖木结构二层楼房，红瓦坡顶，清水砖墙；庭院宽敞，花木扶疏；建筑造型稳重大方，内部装修考究。

原餐厅 Original dining room

The Former Residence of Zhang Xueming sits at No.50 Munan Avenue, Heping District, being the important heritage site under state protection and the special protection historic architecture in Tianjin, and it is used as an office building now. Being the second younger brother of General Zhang Xueliang and son of the warlord Zhang Zuolin, Zhang Xueming (1908–1983) came from Haicheng County of Liaoning Province. In 1928, Zhang Xueming went to study in Japanese Army Infantry School and took a post in the Northeast Army after returning in 1929. He was appointed director of Tianjin Municipal Public Security Bureau in 1930, and Tianjin mayor in April 1931. During his term of office, Zhang Xueming reinforced police work and disciplines, increased facilities. Through the half-year rectification and training, Tianjin policemen became the national model. In March 1931, the newly appointed director of Shenyang Public Security Bureau, Huang

外景 Exterior view

Xiansheng, temporarily transferred policemen from Tianjin to demonstrate in Shenyang Police Station. Under the leadership of Zhang Xueming, Tianjin military policemen defeated riots by Japanese plainclothes policemen twice in 1931. After the foundation of the People's Republic of China, he was appointed as the vice-director of the Tianjin Revolutionary Committee of the Chinese Kuomintang, the commissioner of the Chinese People's Political Consultative Conference, and the member of the Standing Committee of the Tianjin People's Political Consultative Conference.

Built in 1925, this building covers an area of about 1,800 square meters and its floor area is about 1,700 square meters. The brick-wood residence is two-storied with red-tiled sloping roofs and dry brick walls. It has got a giant courtyard with flourishing plants. The building is considered to be a massive and tasteful design along with its elegant interior decorations.

外景 Exterior view

颜惠庆旧宅

Former Residence of Yan Huiqing

颜惠庆旧宅位于和平区睦南道24～26号，全国重点文物保护单位，特殊保护等级历史风貌建筑，建于20世纪20年代，现为办公用房。颜惠庆（1877—1950），上海人，早年就读于美国弗吉尼亚州中学，毕业于该州州立大学。辛亥革命后，颜惠庆历任外交次长及驻德国、丹麦、瑞典等国公使，1919年巴黎和会期间，任中国政府代表团顾问。1920年他升任外交总长，1922年任国务总理兼外交总长，后任财政整理委员会委员长、农商总长、内务总长等职，1927年寓居天津。中华人民共和国成立后，颜惠庆曾任华东军政委员会副主席。

该建筑1943年曾作为伪满洲国领事馆。旧宅占地面积约1 300 m^2，建筑面积约2 400 m^2，三层砖混结构楼房（设有地下室），红瓦坡顶，硫缸砖清水墙面。建筑对称布局，规整大方，硫缸砖墙面的生动肌理和西方古典拱券、柱廊配合得相得益彰，体现了天津地方建筑材料和西洋建筑风格的完美结合。

内景 Inner view

Built in the 1920s, the former Residence of Yan Huiqing is located at No.24~26 Munan Avenue, Heping District, listed as the important heritage site under state protection and the special protection historic architecture in Tianjin. It covers an area of about 1,300 square meters while its floor area is about 2,400 square meters, and the building is used as an office building now. Yan Huiqing (1877–1950) was born in Shanghai. In his early years, he studied in a high school in Virginia, U.S.A. and graduated from the state university. After the Revolution of 1911, he was appointed vice foreign minister, ministers to Germany, Denmark and Sweden etc. During the Paris Peace Conference in 1919, he was consultant in the Chinese government delegation. He was appointed as the chief foreign minister in 1920, prime minister and chief foreign minister in 1922, later chairman of Financial Adjustment Committee, minister of Agriculture and Commerce Department and interior minister. He moved to settle in Tianjin in 1927. After the foundation of the People's Republic of China, he was appointed as the vice-chairman of the East China Military-political Committee.

The building was once used as the consulate of the puppet Manchurian State in 1943. The brick-concrete architecture is three-storied with a basement. It is a symmetrical design with red-tiled sloping roofs and dry walls of quarry tiles, looking well-arranged and tasteful. The active texture of the quarry tile seems to well match with the classical taste of the Western arch and portico, being considered as the perfect combination of the local materials with the Western architectural style.

外景 Exterior view

孙殿英旧宅

Former Residence of Sun Dianying

孙殿英旧宅位于和平区睦南道20～22号，全国重点文物保护单位，特殊保护等级历史风貌建筑，现为办公用房。孙殿英（1889—1948），河南永城人，出身绿林，率乌合之众五六千人活动于豫西一带，后被国民政府收编，曾任国民党第六军团十二军军长。1928年，孙殿英以军事演习为名，炸开清东陵，将乾隆及慈禧陵墓盗掘一空，北京珠宝市场价格为之大跌。“七七事变”后，他被冀察政务委员会任命为冀北民军司令，后任新编第五军军长。抗日战争期间他一度投敌，抗战胜利后，所部被国民党政府收编为第三纵队，他任司令。1947年所部在河南汤阴被中国人民解放军歼灭，孙殿英被俘，1948年病死狱中。

该建筑建于1930年，占地面积约2 800 m^2，建筑面积约2 400 m^2，三层砖木结构楼房（设有地下室）。建筑造型高大舒展、错落有致；内外檐采用拱券窗、矩形窗及绞绳状双柱等元素，富丽堂皇，特色鲜明，具有典型的折中主义建筑特征。

外檐柱饰
Column order under the outer-eaves

The former Residence of Sun Dianying was built at No.20~22 Munan Avenue, Heping District, listed as the important heritage site under state protection and the special protection historic architecture in Tianjin, and used as an office building now. Born in Yongcheng County of Henan Province, Sun Dianying (1889–1948) was one of the warlords, once being a bandit. He led a rabble of 5,000~6,000 people moving in western Henan Province, later incorporated by the government of the Republic of China and he was appointed as the commander of the 12th Army Corps, the sixth Corps Group of Kuomintang Army. Under the plea of a sham battle, his army

外景 Exterior view

blew up the Eastern Tombs of the Qing Dynasty with dynamite, and reaved all the treasures from the tombs of the Empress Dowager Cixi and Emperor Qianlong. The jewel market price in Beijing crashed accordingly. After the Lugouqiao Incident, he was appointed as the commander of Northern Hebei militia by Political Council for Hebei and Chahar, and later commander of the New Fifth Army. During the Anti-Japanese War, Sun Dianying surrendered to the Japanese and his army was incorporated by the Kuomintang government as the Third Column after the success of the war and he was appointed as the commander. His troops were annihilated by the Chinese People's Liberation Army in Tangyin, Henan Province in 1947. Sun Dianying was captured and later died in jail in 1948.

Built in 1930, this brick-wood building is three-storied along with a basement, being massive and well-unfolded, covering an area of about 2,800 square meters and its floor area is about 2,400 square meters. The structures in different heights, windows in shape of arch and rectangle and double columns in shape of twisted rope are arranged perfectly under the inner- and outer-eaves. The architecture looks more magnificent and brilliant, considering its unique eclectic design.

精美的木雕 Exquisite wood-carvings

外景 Exterior view

入口门廊柱头
Column capitals of the portico at the main entrance

纳森旧宅

Former Residence of Nathan

爱德华·乔纳·纳森，英籍犹太人，1910年来华，任职于开平矿务局，1928年后，历任开滦矿务局副总经理、董事部主席兼总经理。纳森在开滦煤矿残酷剥削工人，勾结日军镇压工人运动，引发了开滦五矿大罢工和冀东起义，使矿工们走上了抗日武装斗争的道路。1943年，纳森被解往山东潍县集中营。

纳森旧宅位于和平区睦南道70号，全国重点文物保护单位，特殊保护等级历史风貌建筑，现为办公用房。该建筑建于1928年，占地面积约4 300平方米，建筑面积约1 200平方米，砖木结构庭院式楼房，庭院宽敞，环境幽雅；建筑主体三层，两侧二层，红瓦坡顶，清水砖墙；整体造型不对称，主入口处引导性极强的拱券柱廊成为整个立面的构图中心。

Edward John Nathan, a British Jew, came to China in 1910 and took a position in Kaiping Mining Administration. He was appointed as the General-manager and Board Chairman of the Kailuan Mining Administration from 1928. Nathan exploited workers in Kailuan Coal Mine and suppressed labor movement under the assistance of Japanese troops, causing the Kailuan Strike by Five Coal Mine Workers and Jidong Uprising, which led mine workers onto the road of armed struggle against Japanese troops. In 1943, he was sent to the concentration camp in Wei County, Shandong Province.

As the important heritage site under state protection and the special protection historic architecture in Tianjin, the former residence of Nathan was built in 1928 at No.70 Munan Avenue, Heping District. It covers an area of about 4,300 square meters while its floor area is about 1,200 square meters, and it is used as an office building now. The brick-wood building is a multi-layered house with an elegantly giant garden. Its main structure is three-storied with two-storied wings. This is an unsymmetrical design with its dry walls and the red sloping roofs. The arched portico at the main entrance serves as the central point of the elevations.

雪景 Snow view

旋转楼梯 Spiral stairs

老家具 Old-fashioned furniture

一楼门厅 Inside the entrance

外景 Exterior view

刘冠雄旧宅

Former Residence of Liu Guanxiong

刘冠雄旧宅位于河西区马场道123号，天津市文物保护单位，重点保护等级历史风貌建筑，现为办公用房。刘冠雄（1853—1927），字资颖，福建福州人，毕业于福州船政学堂，后留学英国，回国后任靖远舰帮统。1894年参加中日甲午海战，后任海天舰管带、德州兵工厂总办等职。辛亥革命后，他先后九次出任北洋政府海军总长，后寓居天津。

该建筑建于1922年，占地面积约3 700 m^2，建筑面积约1 600 m^2，砖木结构三层楼房，设有地下室。平面造型类似双筒望远镜，体现了主人的身份和魂寄海军的情怀。立面清水红砖墙与混水线条装饰相搭配，生动清新。室内装饰豪华大气，布局合理，使用功能齐全。

Located at No.123 Machang Avenue, Hexi District, the former Residence of Liu Guanxiong is the heritage site under city protection and the important protection historic architecture and is now an office building. Liu Guanxiong (1853–1927), with a courtesy name of Ziying, was born in Fuzhou, Fujian Province. After graduating from Fuzhou Arsenal Naval College, he went to study in the U.K., and was appointed as the vice battalion commander on Cruiser Jingyuan after returning to China. In 1894, he joined the Sino-Japanese War of 1894–1895 and then was appointed as the captain of Cruiser Haitian and the director of Dezhou Arsenal, etc. After the Revolution of 1911, he was named Chief of Navy by the Beiyang Government for nine times and settled in Tianjin later.

The three-storied brick-timber building with basements was constructed in 1922, covering an area of about 3,700 square meters and a floor area of about 1,600 square meters. The horizontal modeling is like a binocular, presenting the owner's status and his affection on navy. The wall was built by fair-faced red bricks, decorated by furred lines vividly and freshly. The interior finish is luxurious, elegant, well-arranged and fully-functioned .

外景 Exterior view

一楼大厅 Lobby on the first floor

三层楼梯间
Staircase of the third floor

疙瘩楼

Knotty Building

疙瘩楼位于和平区河北路283～295号，全国重点文物保护单位，重点保护等级历史风貌建筑，现为居住、商业用房。疙瘩楼为英商先农公司于1937年建造的独户联排公寓，占地面积约1 900 m^2，建筑面积约2 900 m^2，由意大利建筑师鲍乃弟设计。砖木结构三层楼房，设有半地下室作为车库。建筑平面布局合理，采用当时欧洲流行的联排独户住宅的布局，是当时中产阶级的理想住宅。建筑依街角设计，与地形结合较好。建筑外檐为红瓦坡屋顶，硫缸砖清水墙面。建筑巧妙使用天津地方材料——硫缸砖，整个墙面上不均匀的凸起呈“疙瘩”状，别具特色，故称“疙瘩楼”。同时在每户住宅的入口、悬挑阳台、檐部、窗间墙和窗套等处，采用拱券、花纹、水纹等古典和洛可可式装饰手法，使得建筑整体简洁大方，细部浪漫和谐。室内装修考究，木地板、木楼梯、木门窗等保存完好。著名京剧大师马连良曾在此居住。

外景 Exterior view

外檐局部 Partial outer-eaves

Located at No.283~295 Hebei Road of Heping District, Knotty Building is the important heritage site under state protection and the important protection historic architecture, and now used as a residential and commercial building. Built in 1937 by British Xiannong Company, the single-family attached apartment building covers an area of 1,900 square meters and a floor area of 2,900 square meters. Designed by the Italian architect, Paul Bonetti, the three-storied building is a brick-timber structure with a semi-basement as garage. The building's layout is reasonable, applying the popular single-family attached residence mode then. It is an ideal residence for the middle class. Standing on the corner of the road, the building has a perfect design to suit the landform. It has red-tiled sloping roofs and glazed quarry tiled fair-faced walls. The local material, glazed quarry tile, is skillfully utilized, making the walls protruded with uneven lumps, which is very unique and this is how it gets the name. Meanwhile, arches, decorative patterns and other classic Rococo decorative techniques are applied to the entrance of each household, cantilevered balcony, eaves, walls between windows and window frames, which makes the building brief and elegant on the whole while romantic and harmonious in details. The inner decoration is fancy with the wooden floors, staircases, doors and windows well preserved. The famous Peking opera master, Ma Lianliang, once lived here.

安乐邨
Anle Village

安乐邨位于和平区马场道与桂林路交口，共三幢联排式公寓住宅，呈“品”字形分布，一幢平行马场道为三层，另两幢垂直马场道为二层，全国重点文物保护单位，均为重点保护等级历史风貌建筑，现为居住、办公和商业用房。建筑建于1933年，占地面积约7 600 m^2，总建筑面积约9 300 m^2，由意大利鲍乃第建筑师事务所设计，英国天主教会首善堂投资建造，当时租给美国武官居住，名为“新武官胡同”，1953年改为现用名称。著名实业家李烛尘曾在此居住。建筑为砖木结构楼房，设有地下室，均由分户单元联排组成，每户前后设小院，平面功能布局合理，厨卫设备齐全。外檐为清水砖墙，坡屋顶，瓦屋面，正立面部分混水抹灰。建筑装饰元素丰富，每户主入口门及二层窗为拱券式，上以西班牙半圆拱花饰装饰。窗间多用绞绳柱支撑，装饰效果较强，使建筑富于韵律感。阳台出挑，下以雕花状牛腿支撑。室内房间设置齐全，暖卫设施完备，木楼梯、木地板、木门窗至今保持着良好的使用功能。建筑整体具有折中主义建筑特征。

外檐窗
Windows under the outer-eaves

Located at the crossing of Machang Avenue and Guilin Road of Heping District, Anle Village is constituted by three attached apartment buildings, forming an isosceles triangle. The building paralleling Machang Avenue has three stories while the other two perpendicular to Machang Avenue have two stories. Being the important heritage site under state protection and the important protection historic architectures, now they are all residential, office and commercial buildings. Built in 1933, they cover an area of 7,600 square meters and a total floor area of 9,300 square meters. They were designed by Italian Bonetti Partnership Architects and French Catholic Institution, invested by British Catholic. It was named New Military Officer Lane and rent to American military officers. In 1953, its name changed to Anle Village. Li Zhuchen, the famous industrialist, once lived here. The architectures are brick-timber structures with basements, constituted by multi-family units attaching to each other. Each unit has its own front yard and back yard, rational layout and complete kitchen and sanitary facilities. The buildings have fair-faced external walls, sloping roofs with tiles and partial plastered bricks of front elevation walls. Decorative techniques were abundant, including arched main entrance of each unit, arched windows on the second floor, with Spanish semi-circle floriation; twisted columns propping between windows which have a good decorative effect and make the architecture rhythmical; projected balconies propped with engraving corbels. The rooms have complete heating and sanitary facilities. The wooden staircases, floors, doors and windows are well preserved. The buildings have the features of eclectic architecture.

外景 Exterior view

图书在版编目（CIP）数据

天津历史风貌建筑：汉英对照/天津市历史风貌建筑保护专家咨询委员会，天津市保护风貌建筑办公室主编. —天津：天津大学出版社，2017.9（2024.4重印）
ISBN 978-7-5618-5824-0

Ⅰ. ①天… Ⅱ. ①天… ②天… Ⅲ. ①古建筑－介绍－天津市 Ⅳ. ①K928.71

中国版本图书馆CIP数据核字（2017）第237095号

图书策划　金　磊
策划编辑　韩振平工作室　韩振平　朱玉红
责任编辑　郭　颖
装帧设计　谷英卉　董秋岑　康　洁

出版发行　天津大学出版社
地　　址　天津市卫津路92号天津大学内（邮编：300072）
电　　话　发行部：022－27403647
网　　址　publish.tju.edu.cn
印　　刷　北京华联印刷有限公司
经　　销　全国各地新华书店
开　　本　230mm × 300mm
印　　张　18.25
字　　数　220千
版　　次　2017年9月第1版
印　　次　2024年4月第2次
定　　价　188.00元